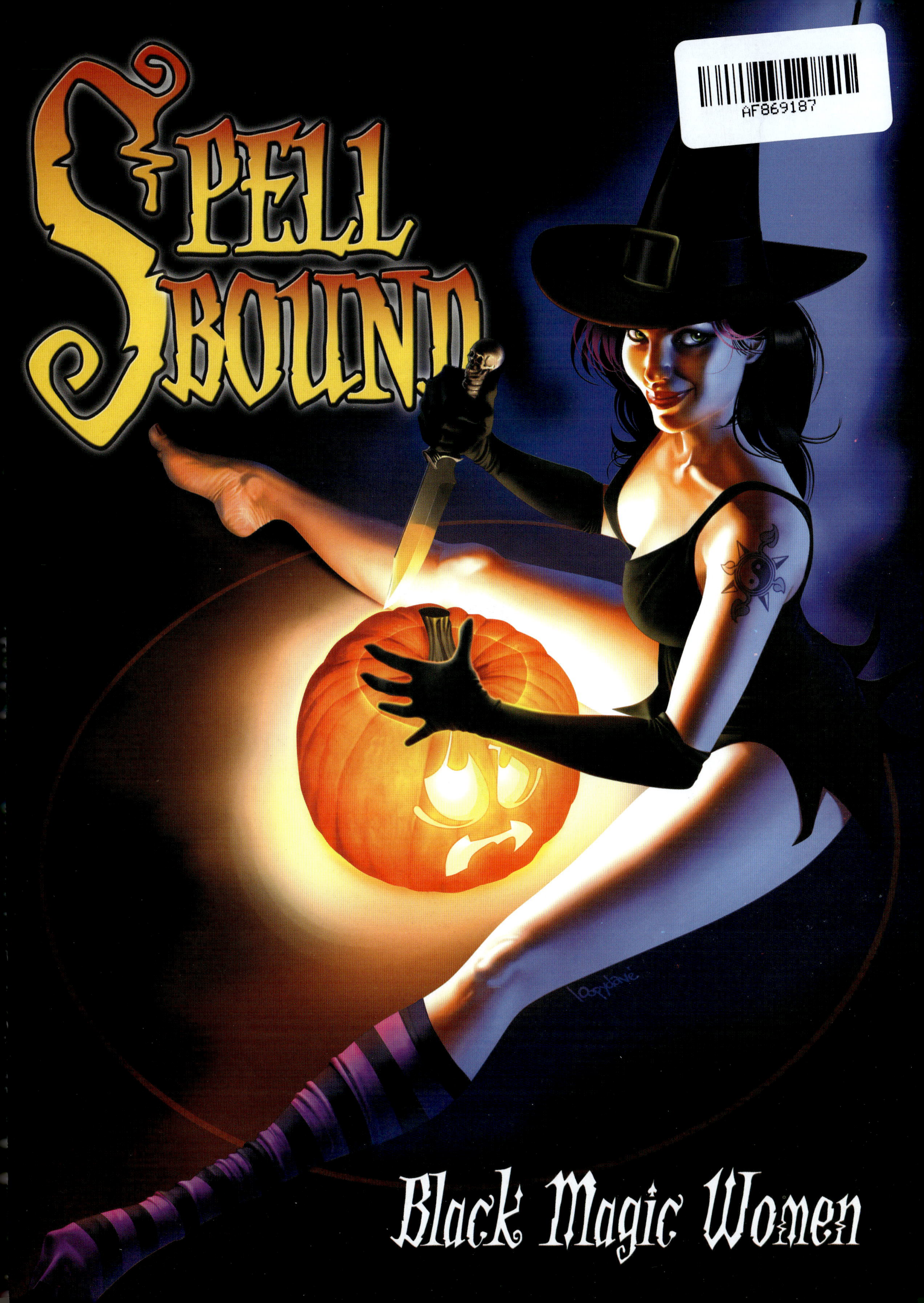
Spell Bound
Black Magic Women

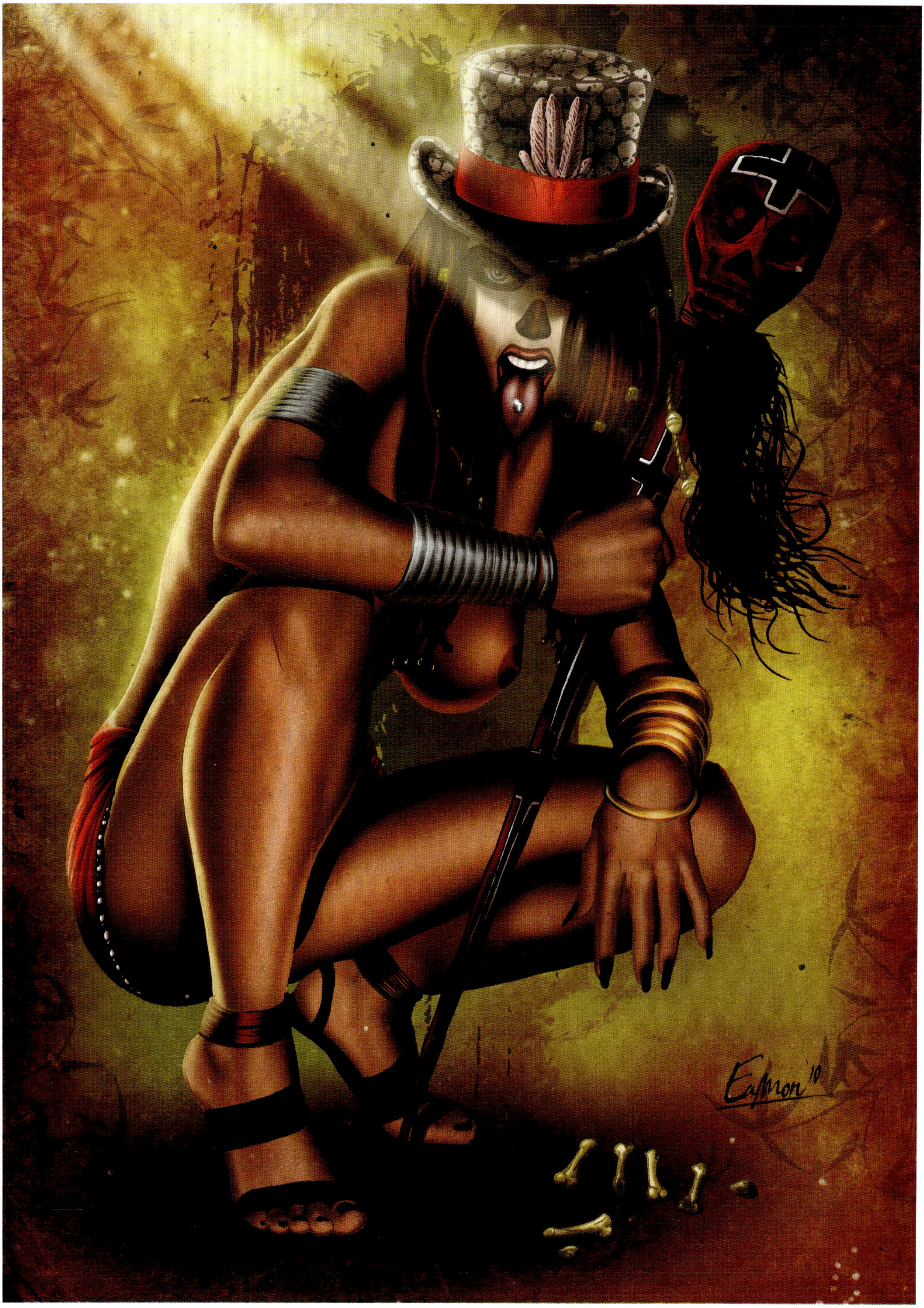

EAMON O'DONOGHUE

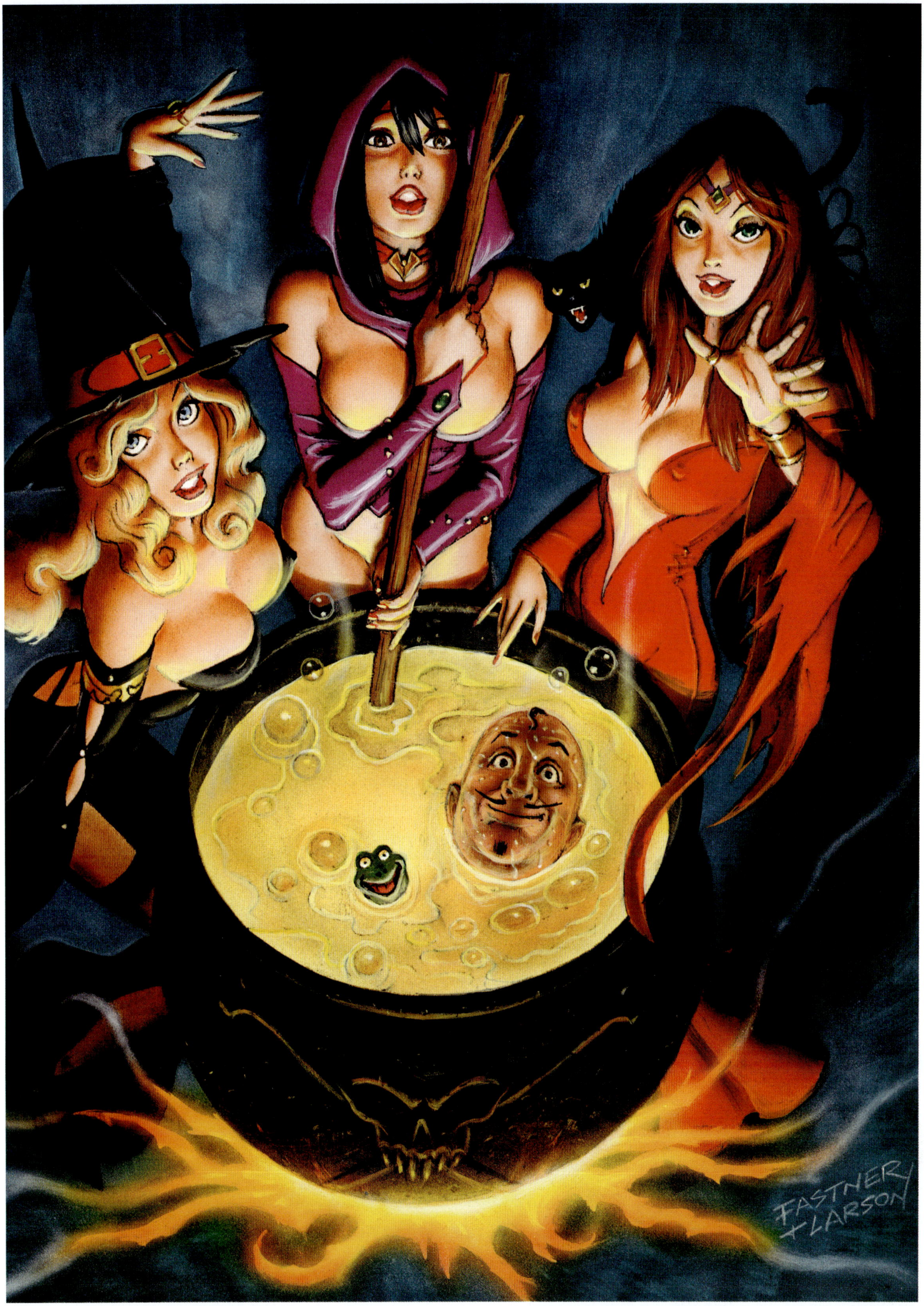

STEVE FASTNER & RICH LARSON

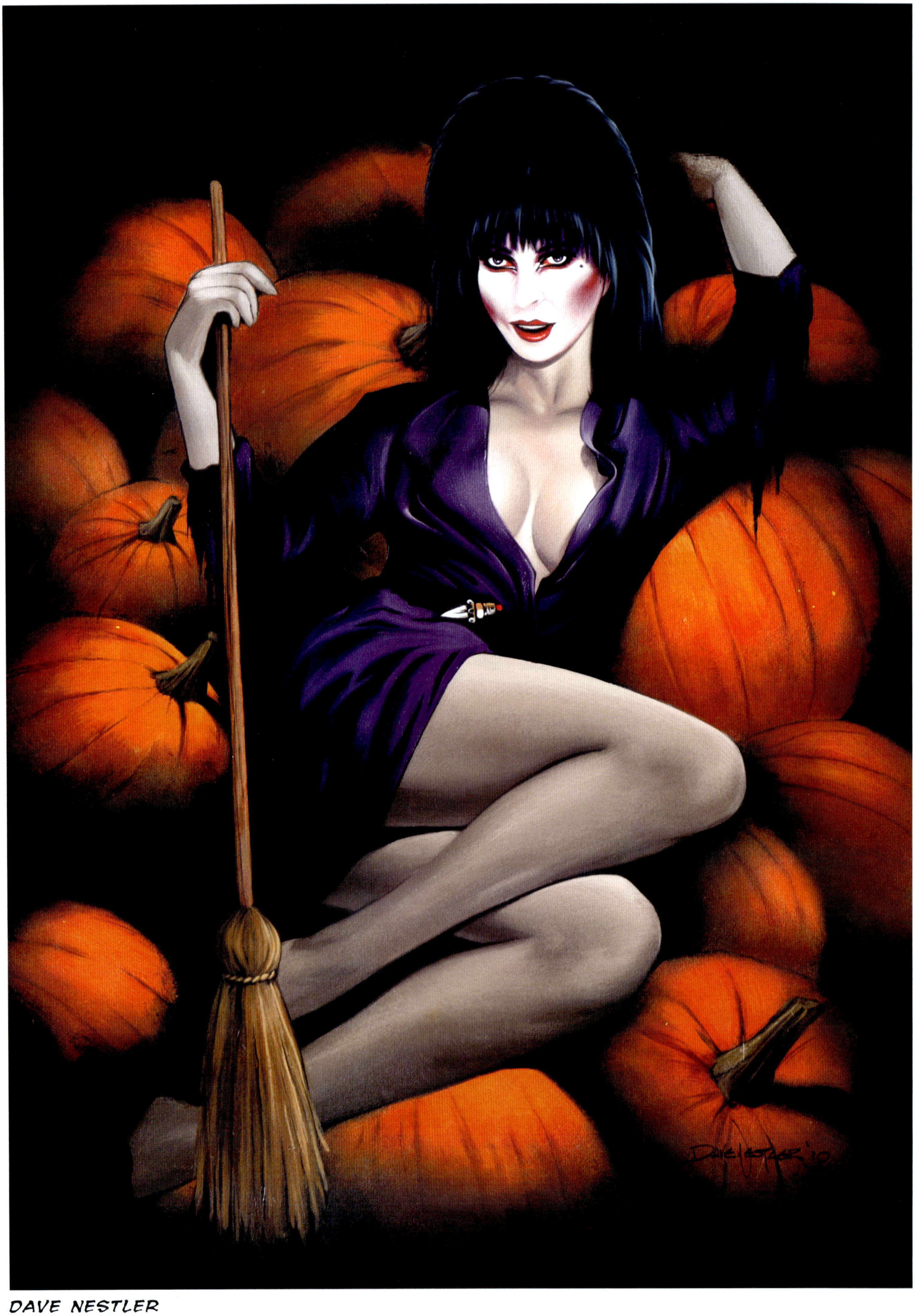

DAVE NESTLER

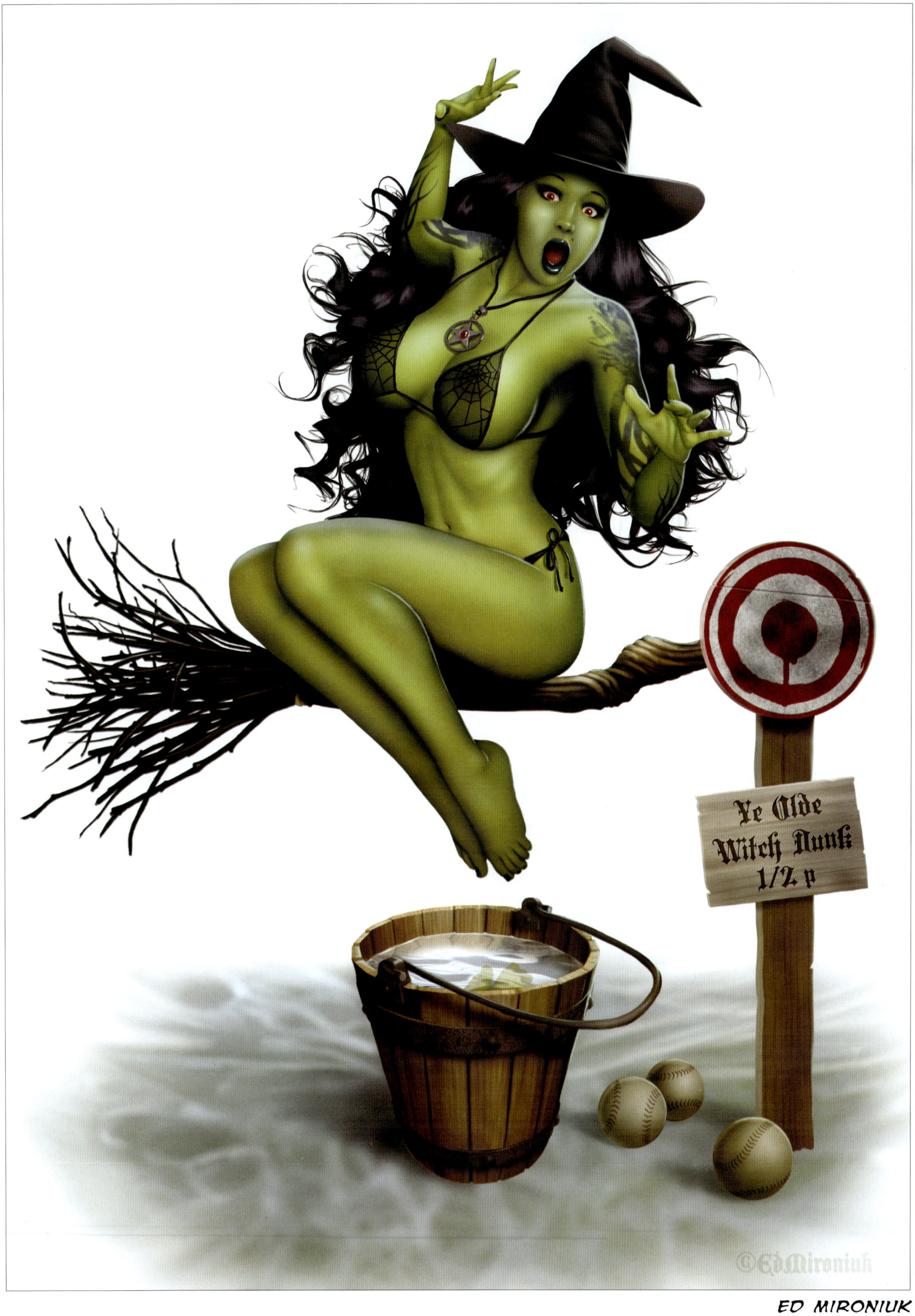

ED MIRONIUK

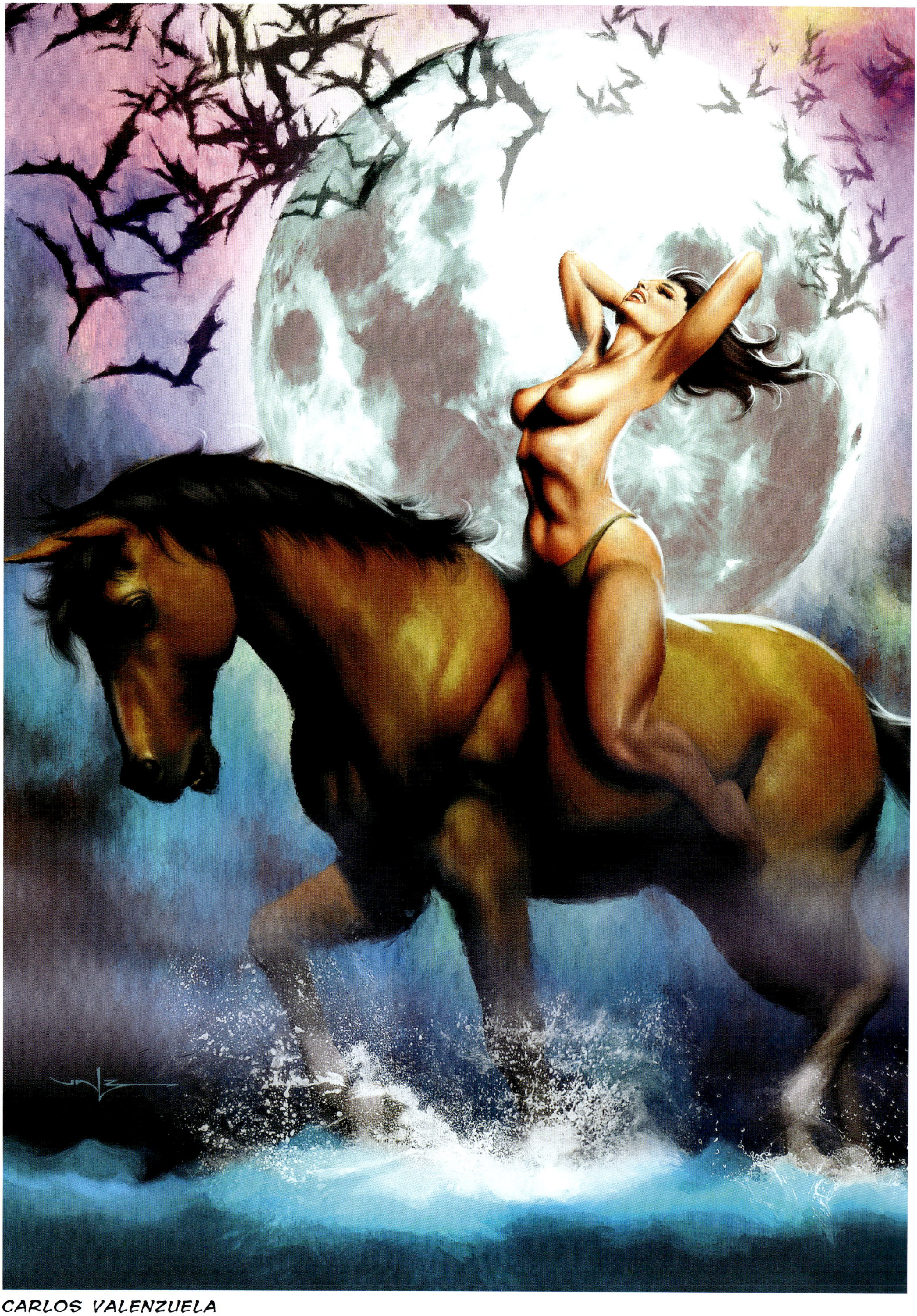

CARLOS VALENZUELA

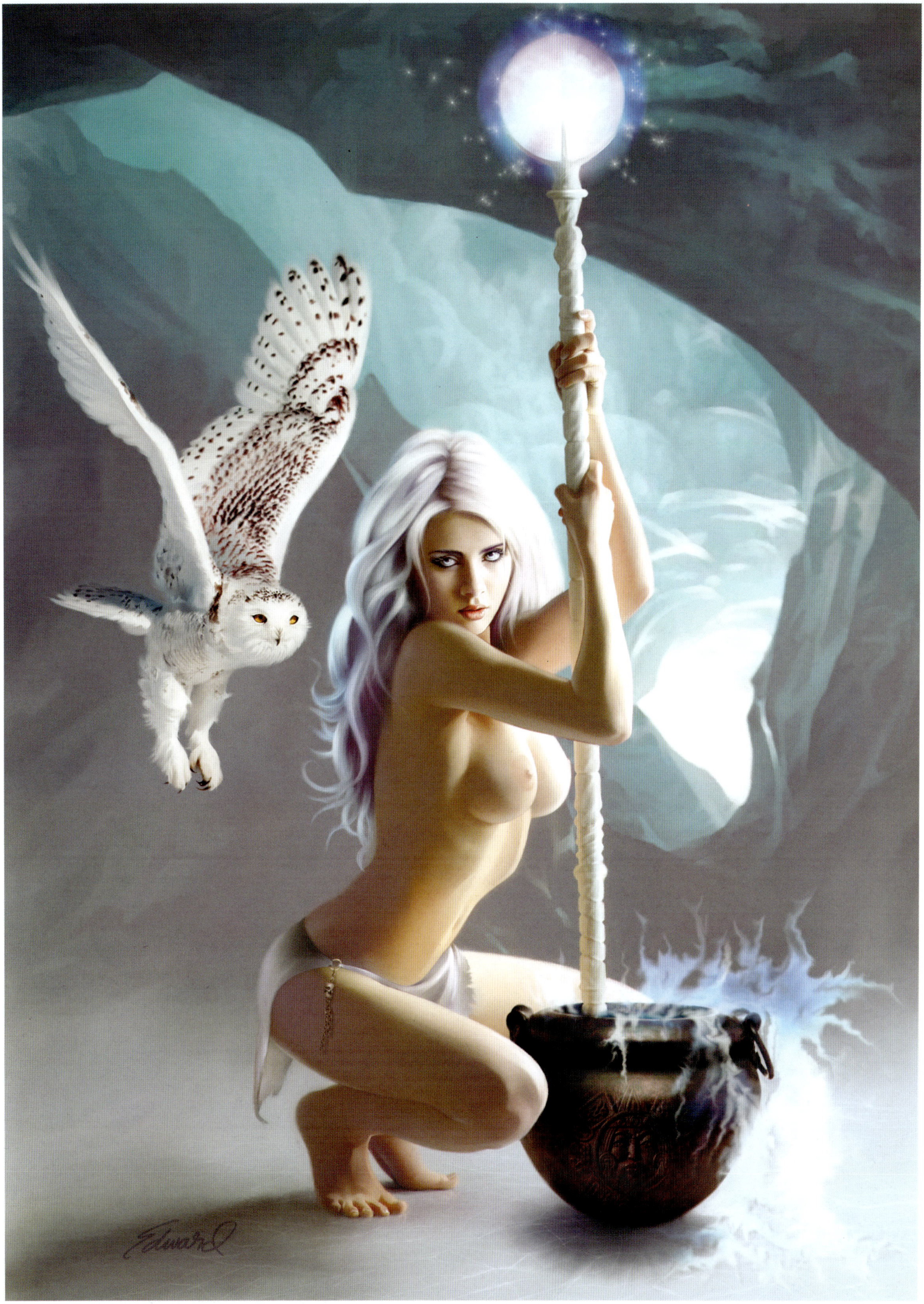

EDWARD REED

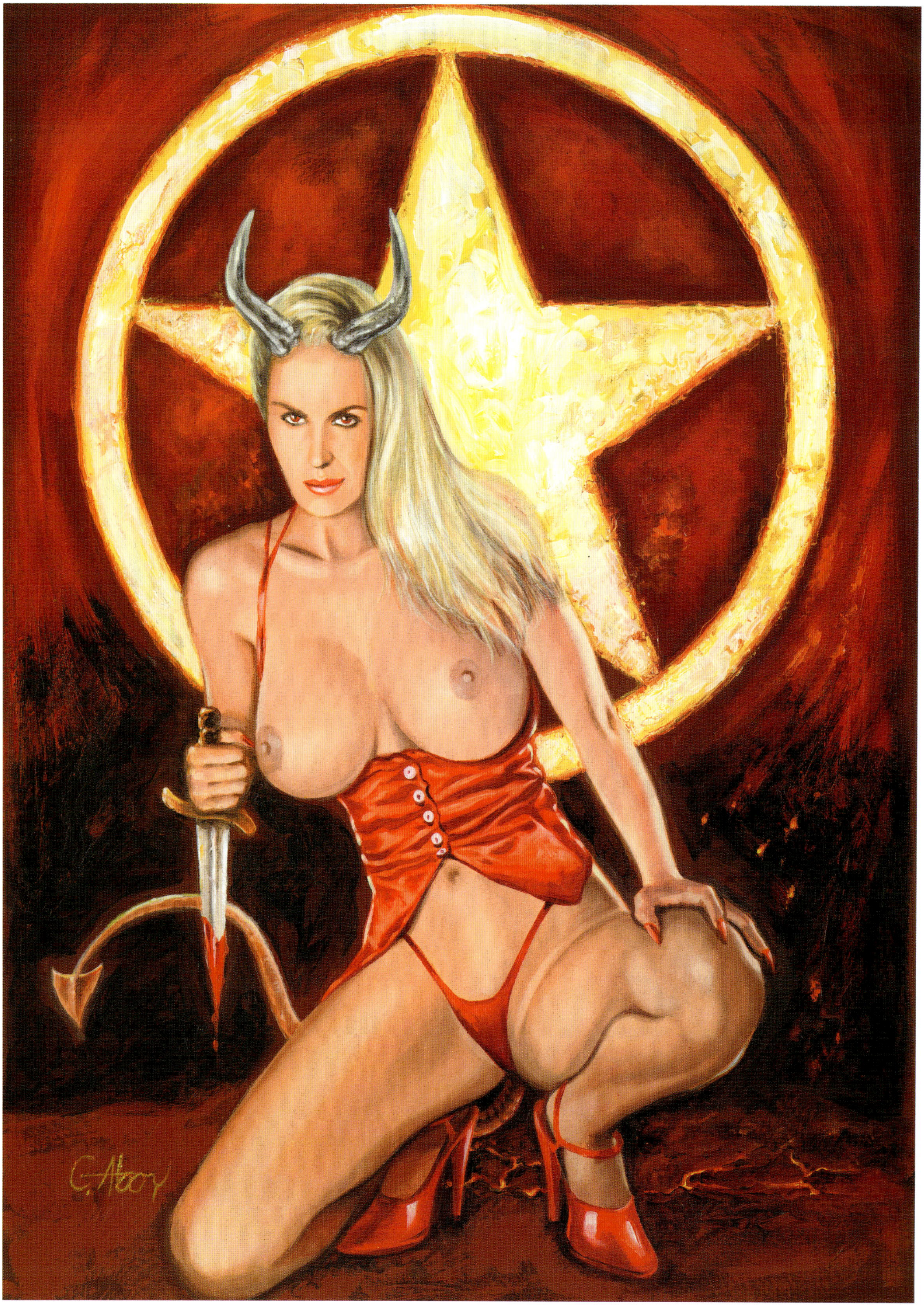

CLAUDIO ABOY

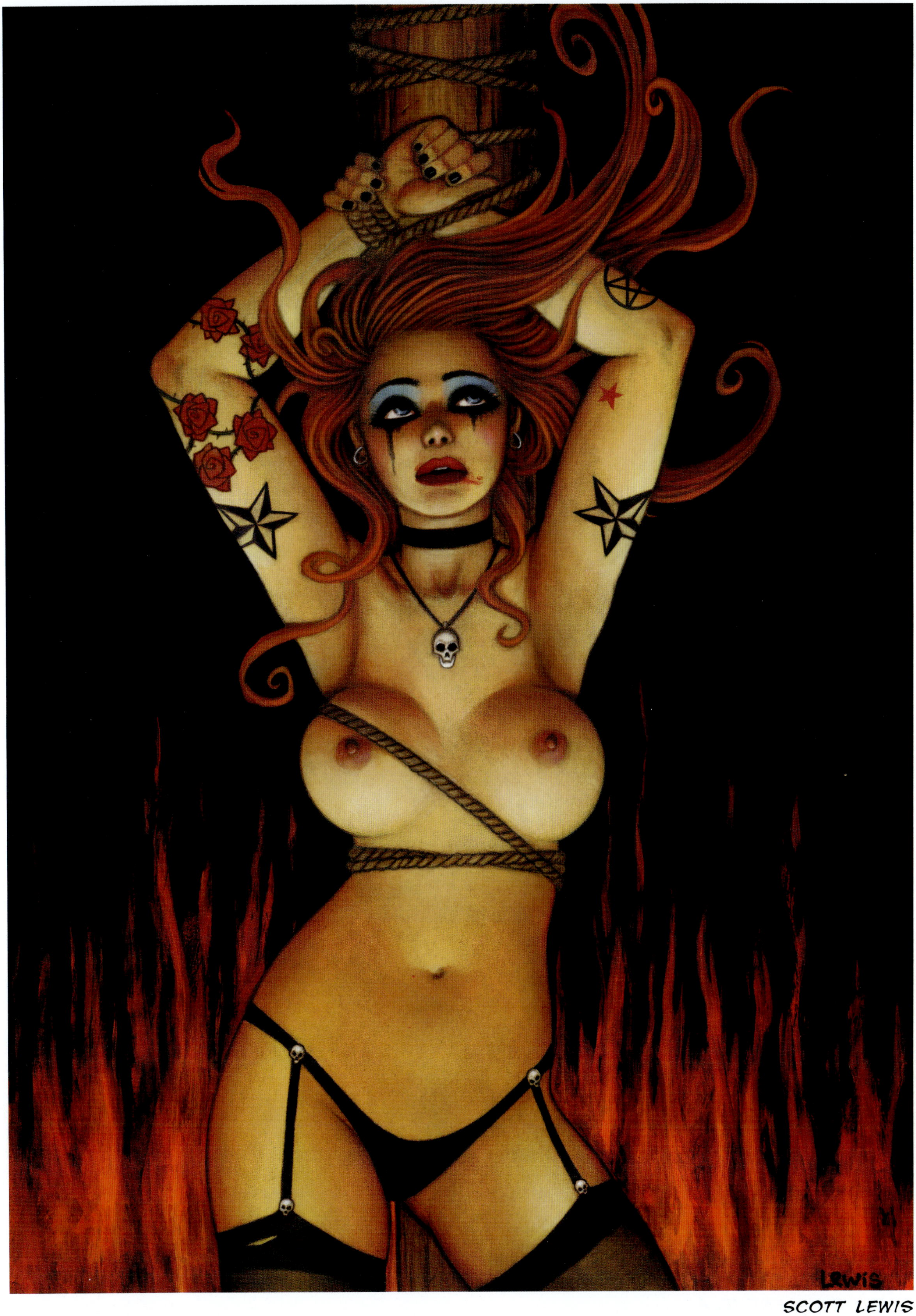

SCOTT LEWIS

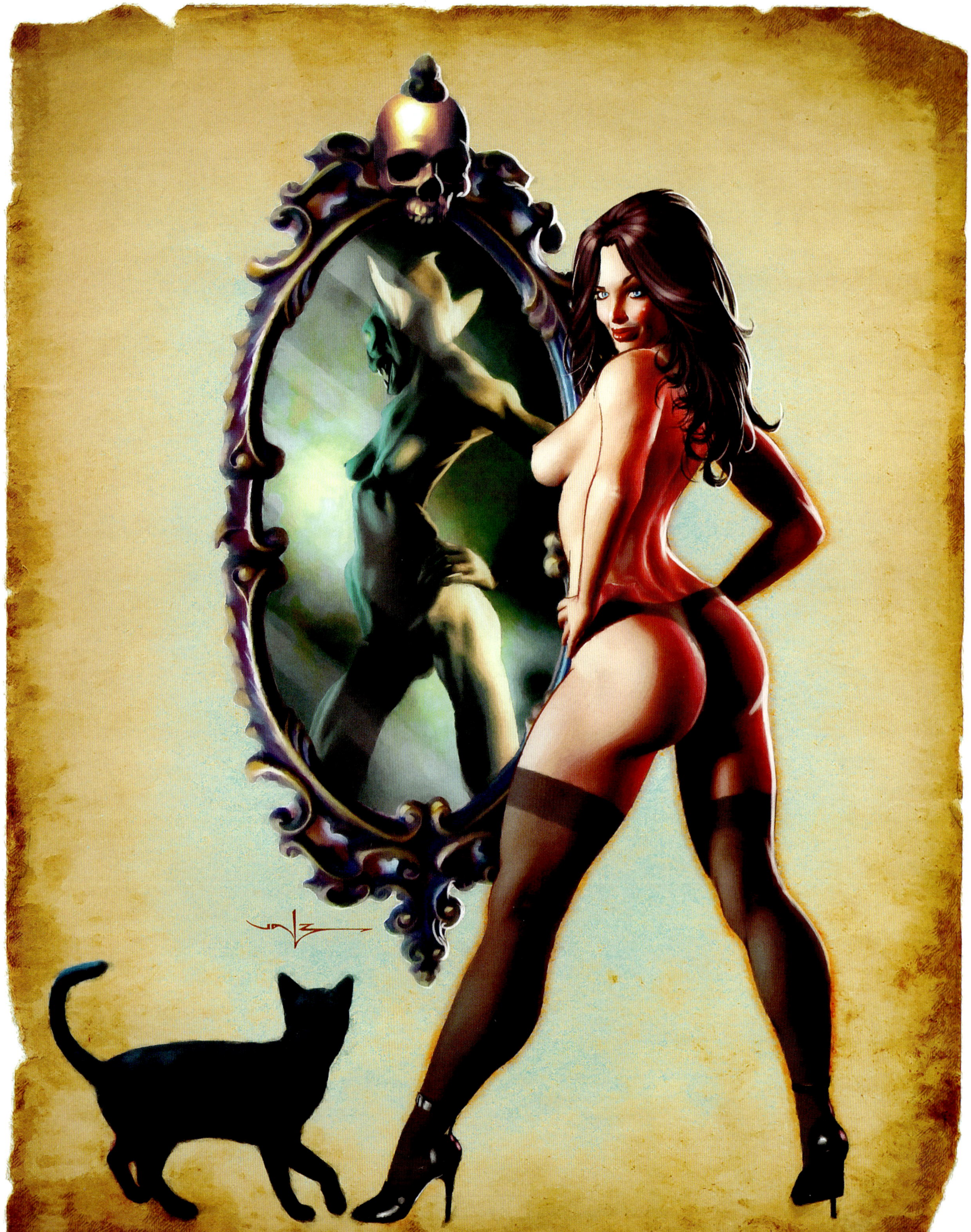

CARLOS VALENZUELA

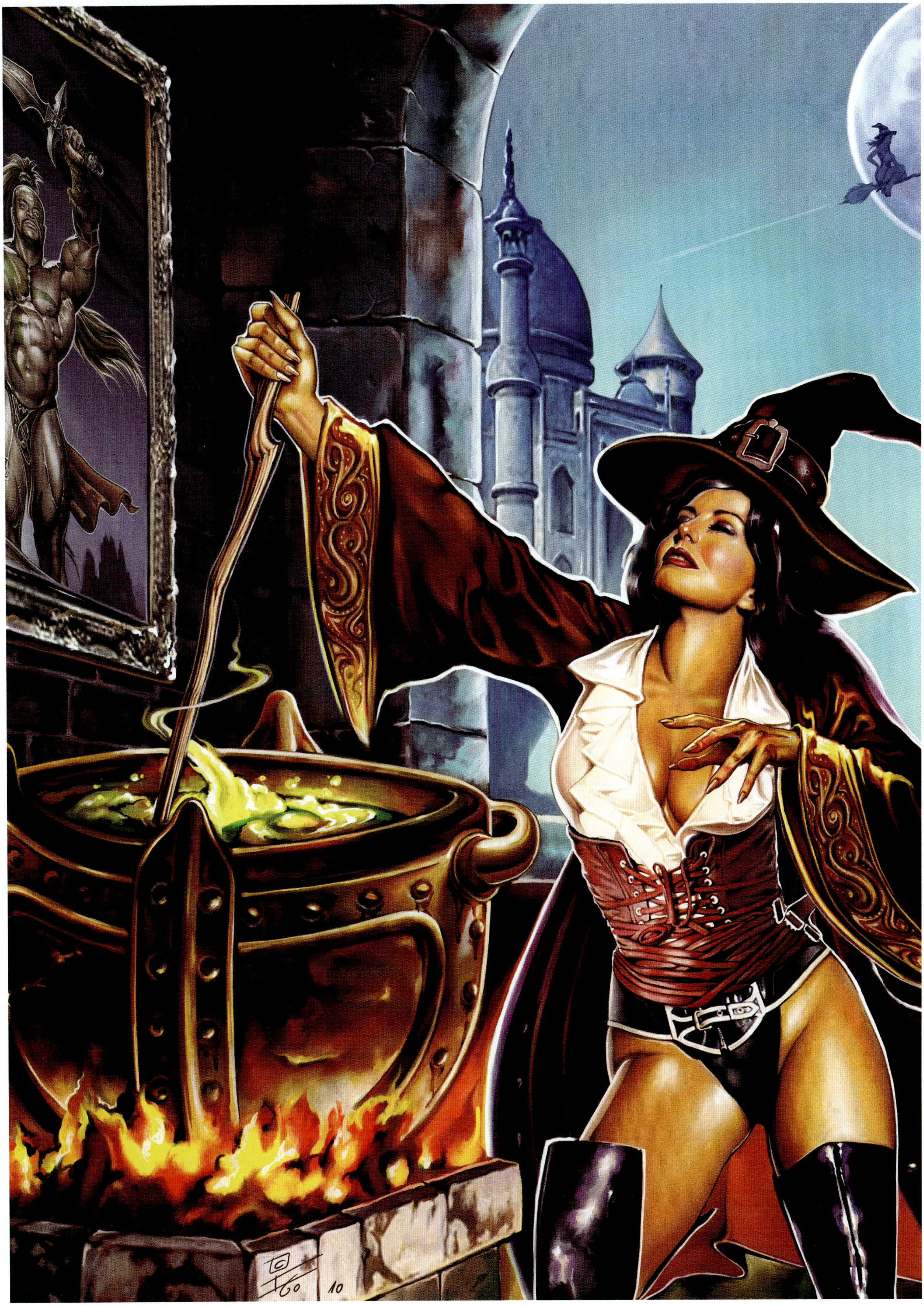

INAKI ORMAETXEA

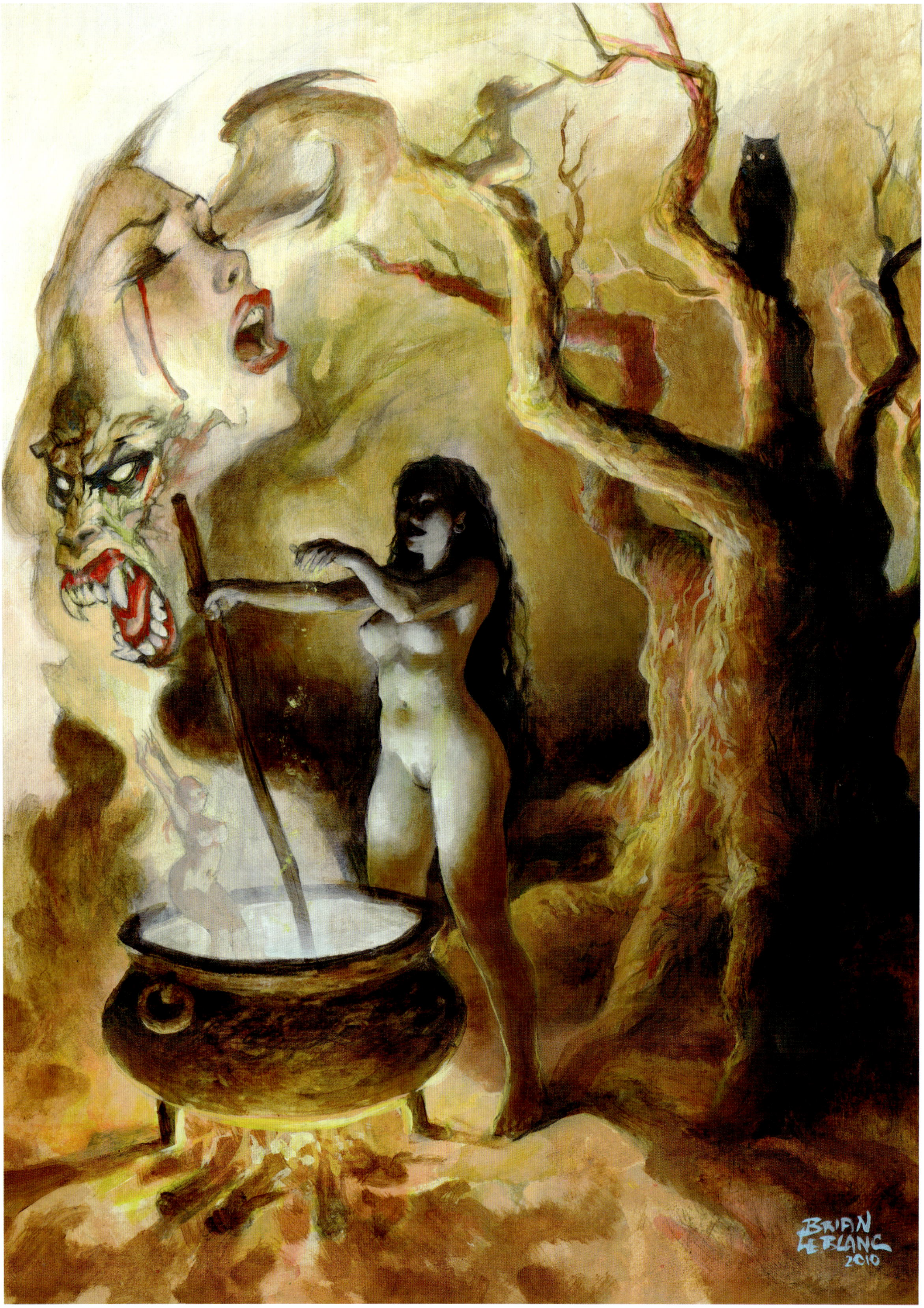

BRIAN LEBLANC

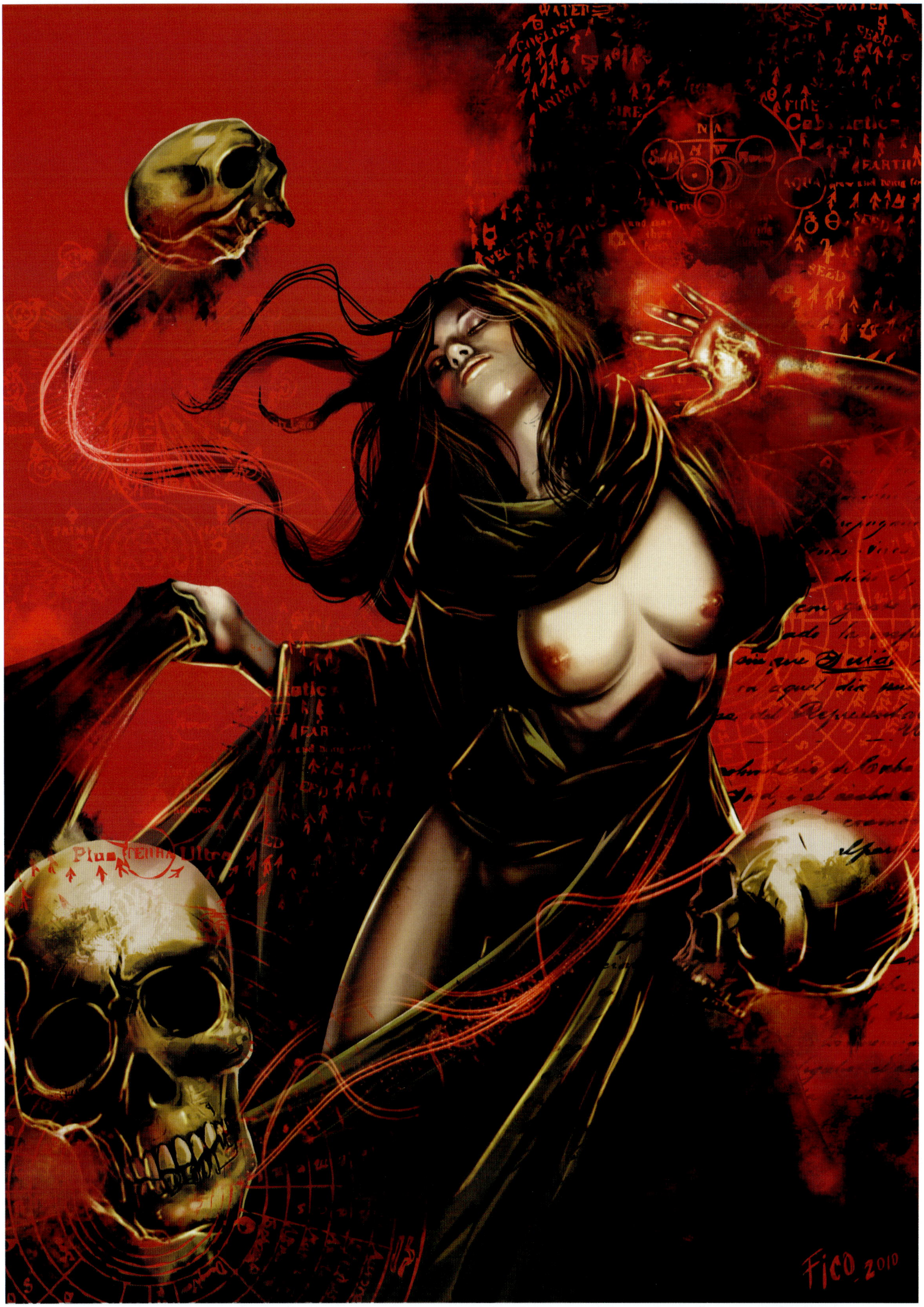

FEDERICO OSSIO

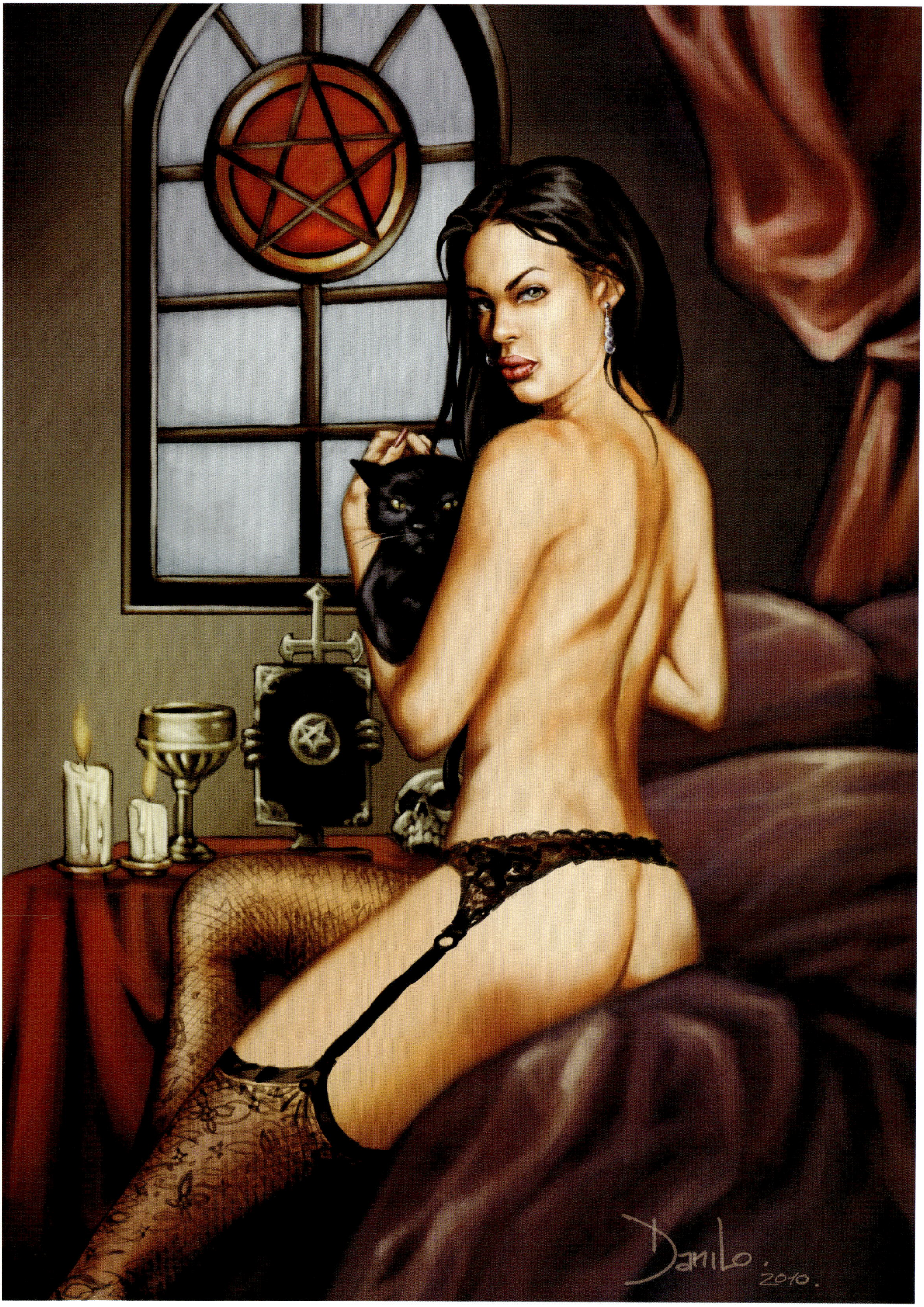

DANILO GUIDA

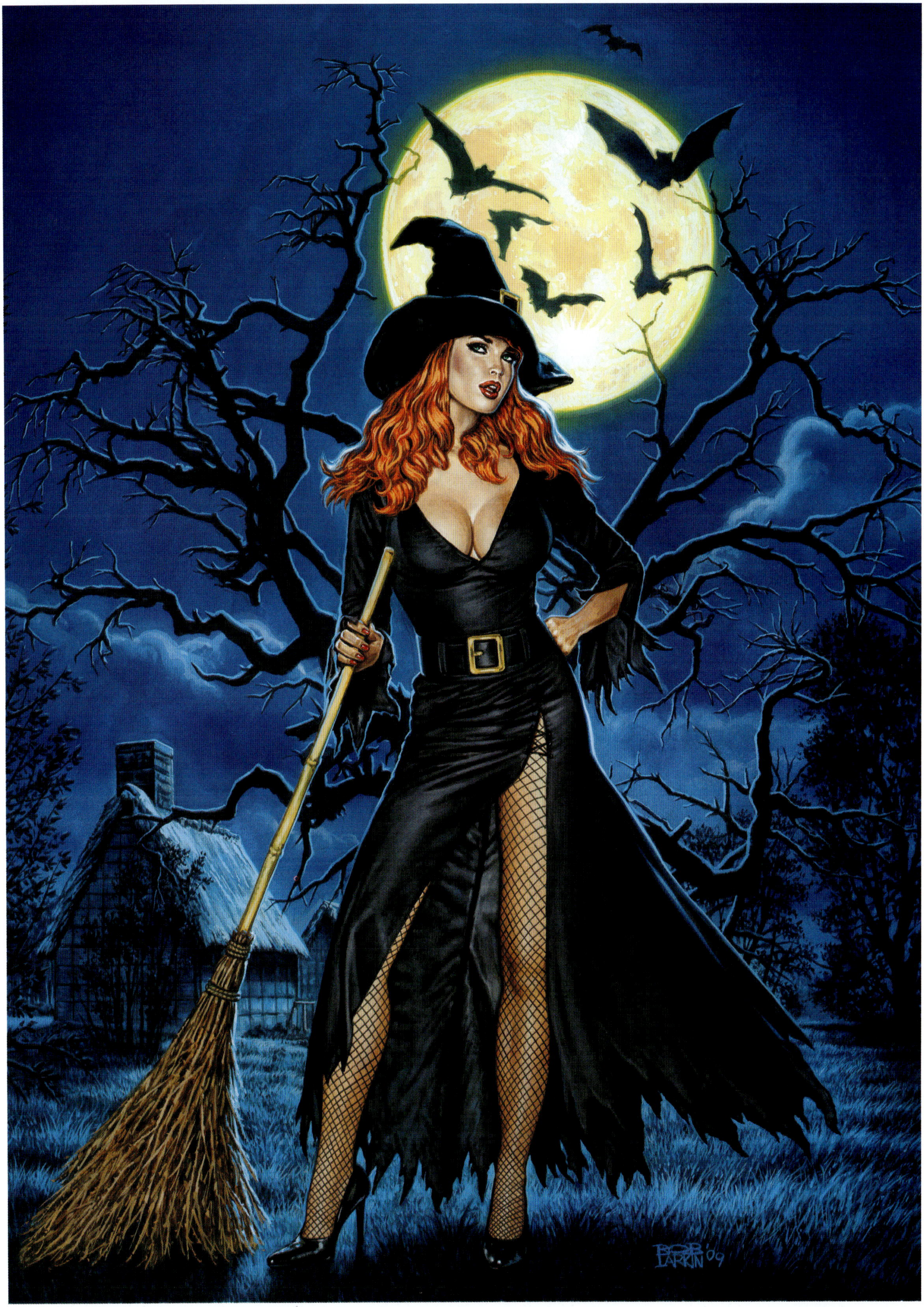

BOB LARKIN

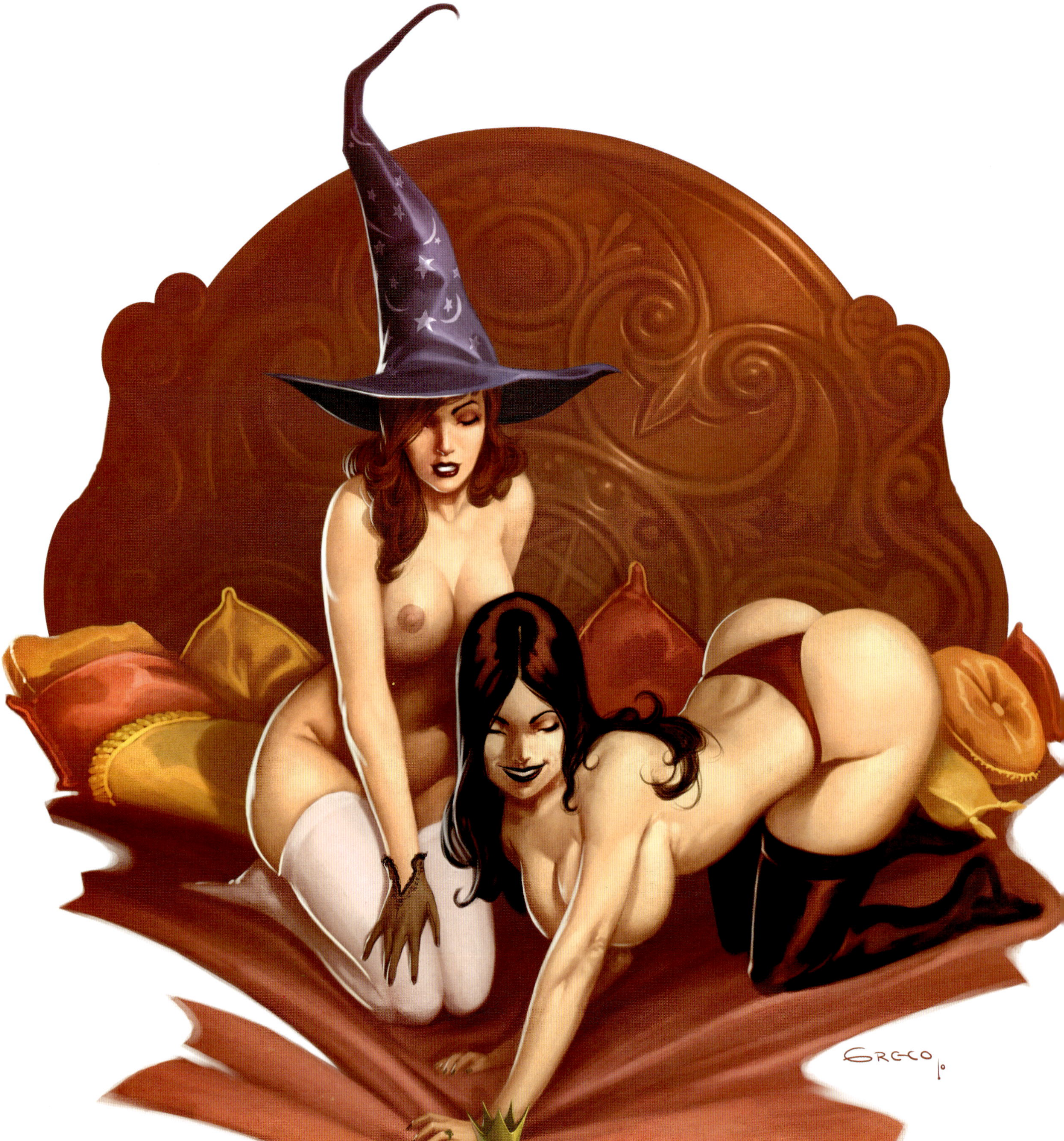

DIEGO GRECO

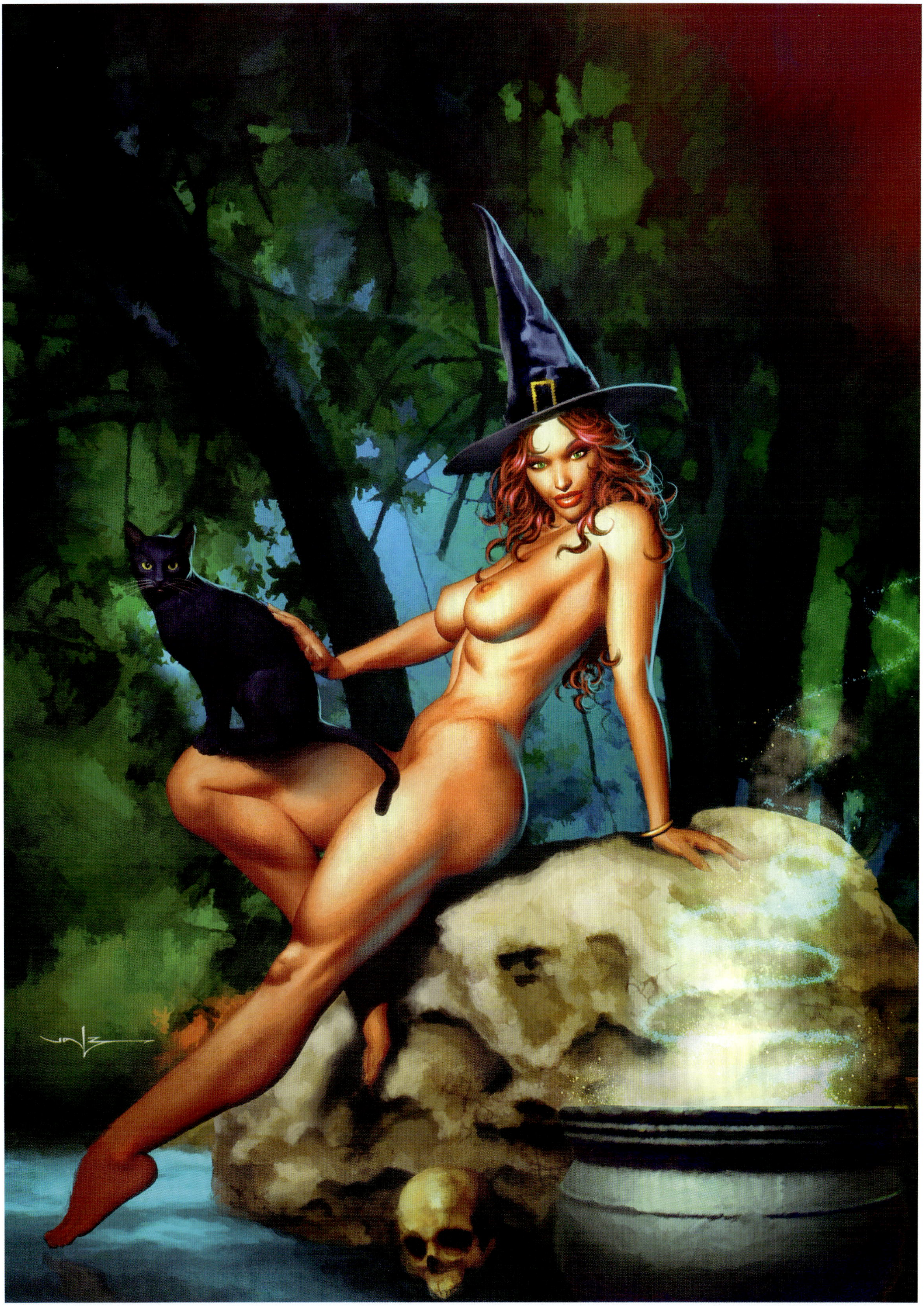

CARLOS VALENZUELA

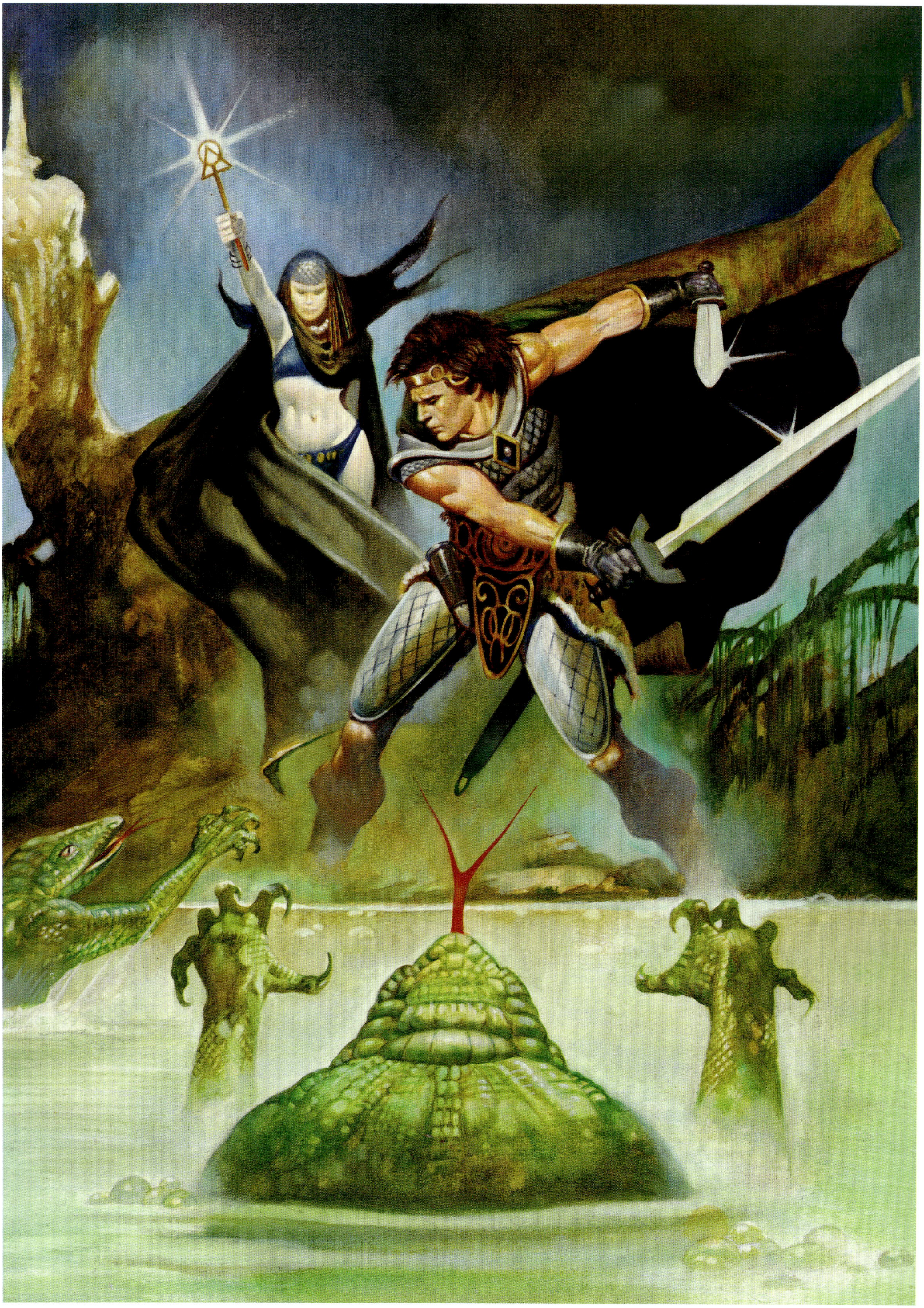

LUIS ROCA

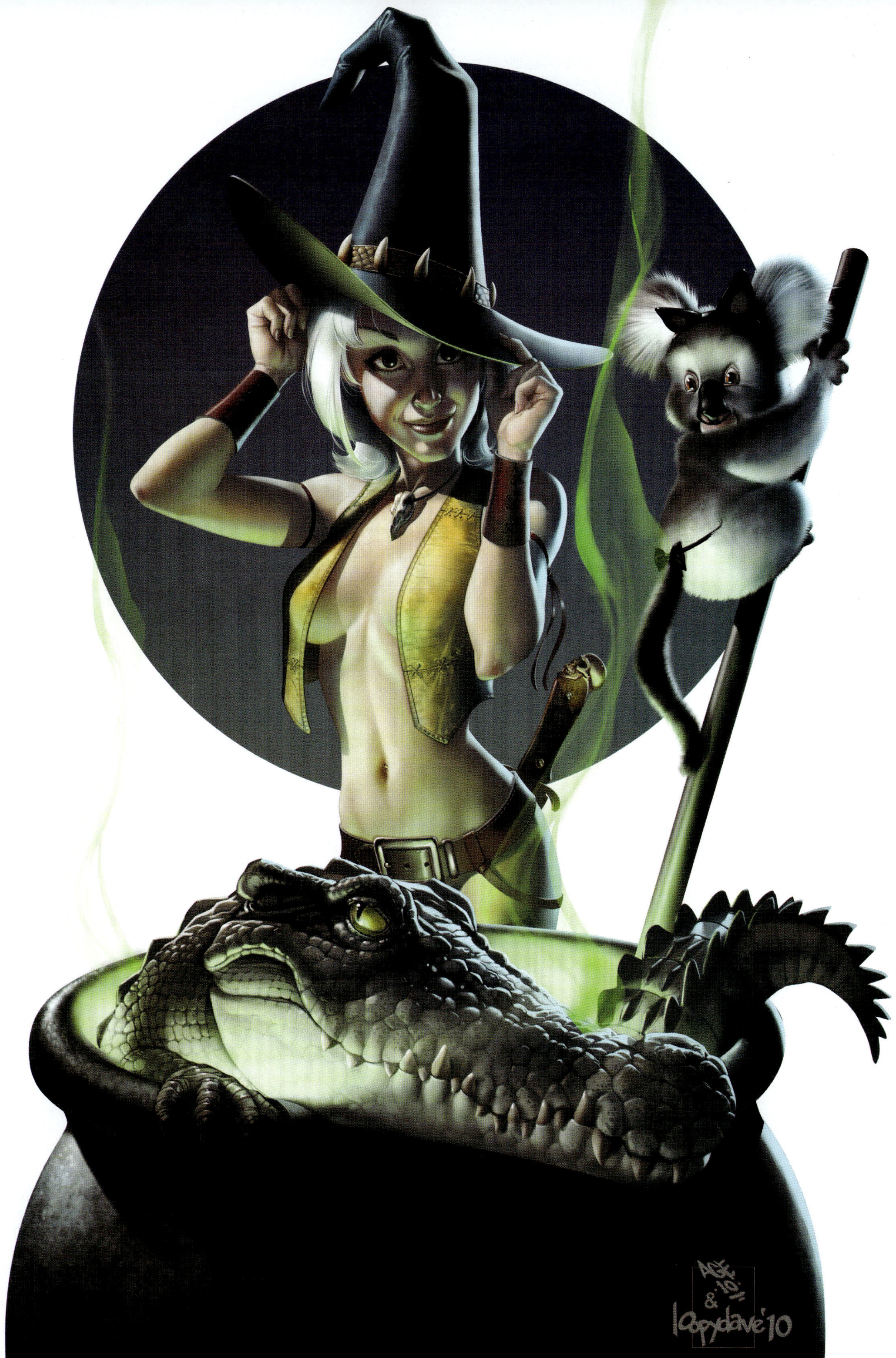

ADRIAN VELEZ & DAVE DUNSTAN

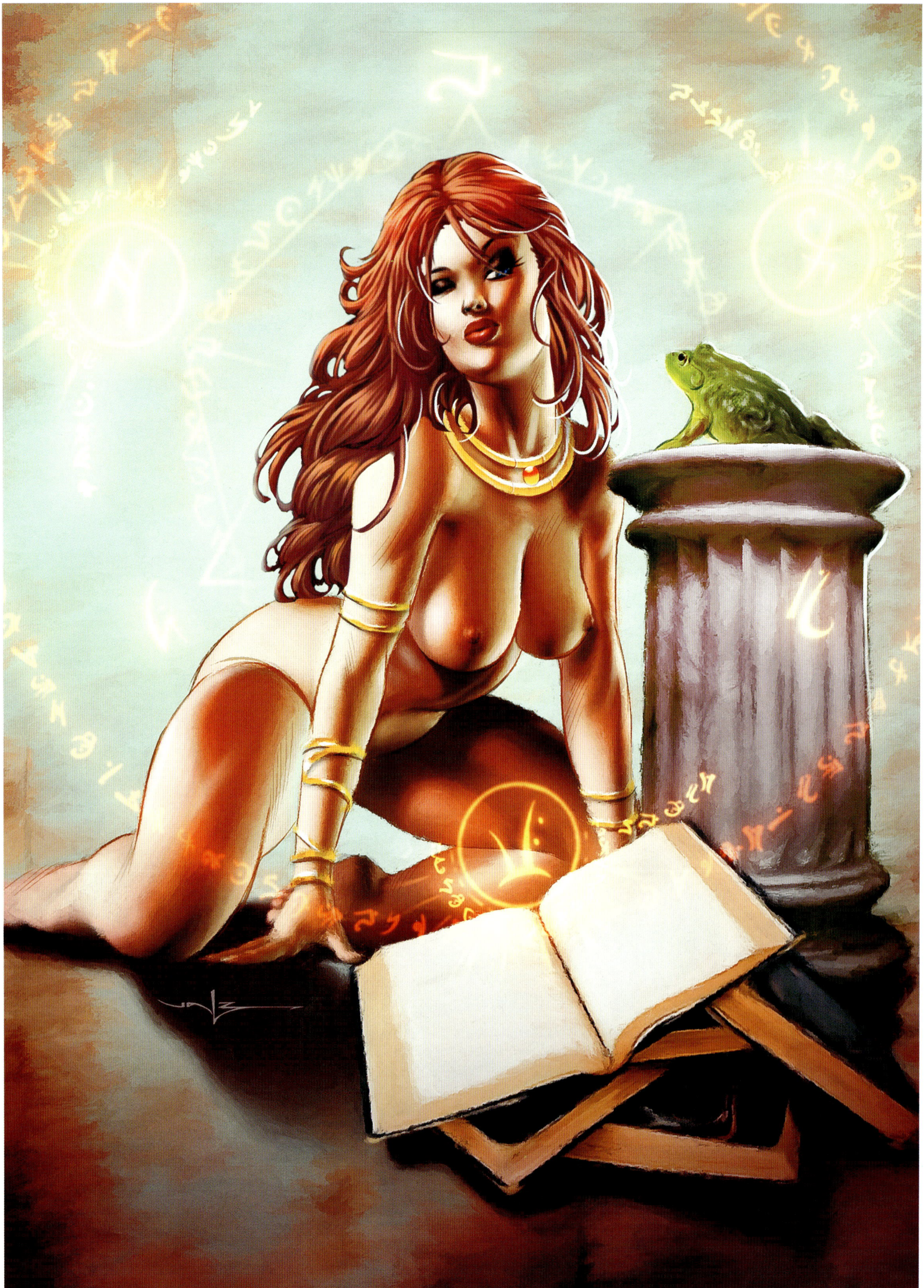

CARLOS VALENZUELA

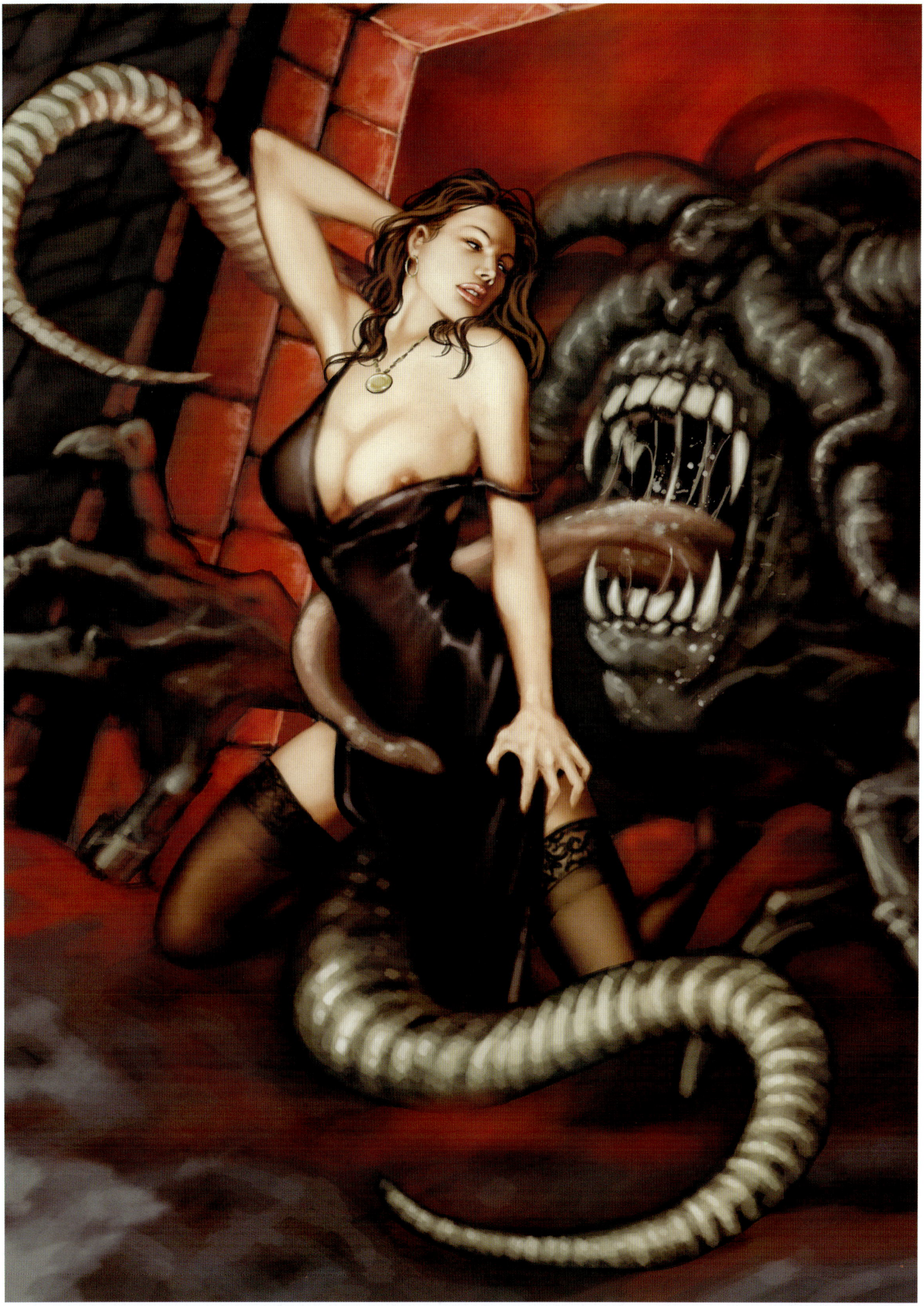

DANILO GUIDA

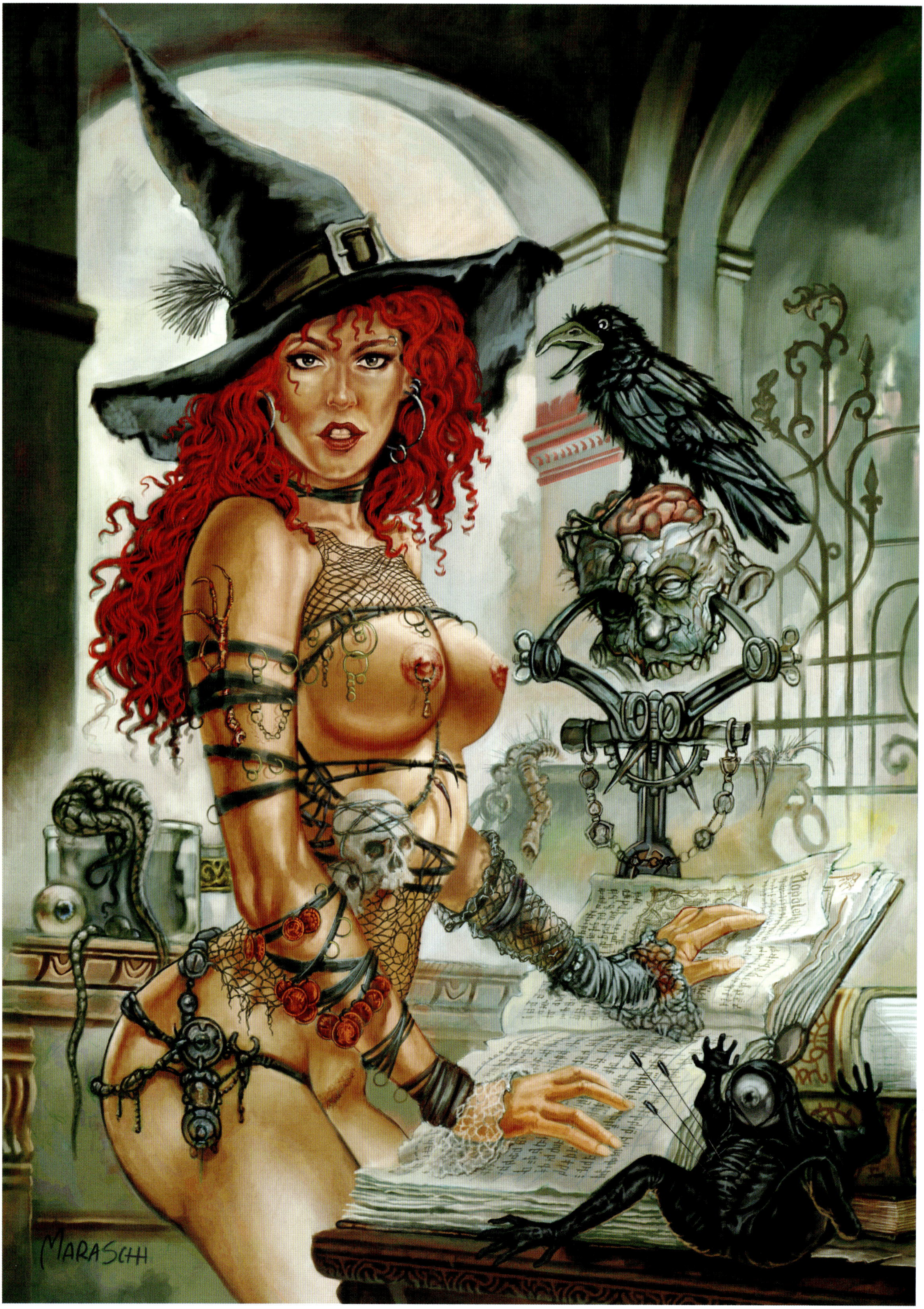

ANIBAL MARASCHI

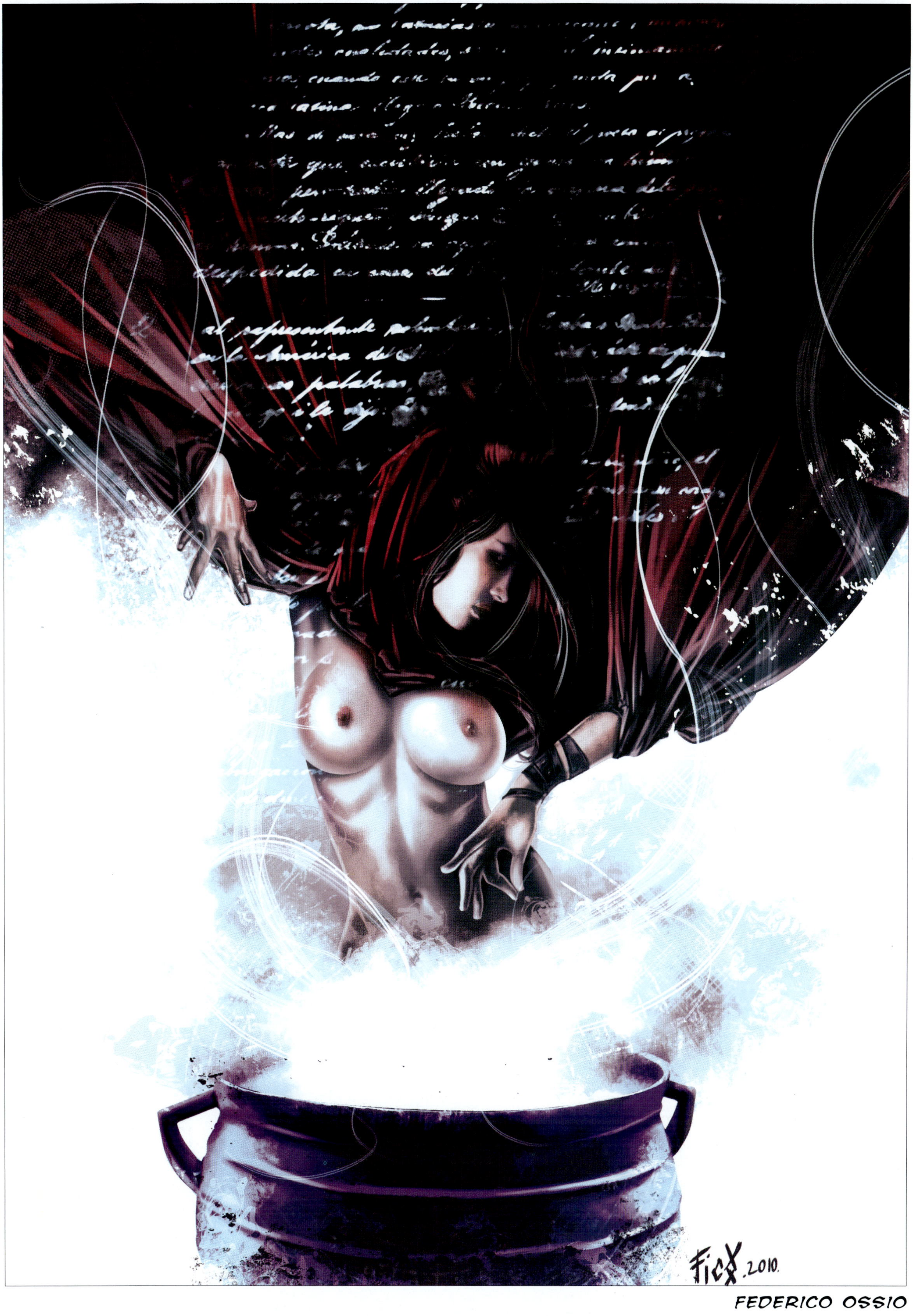

FEDERICO OSSIO

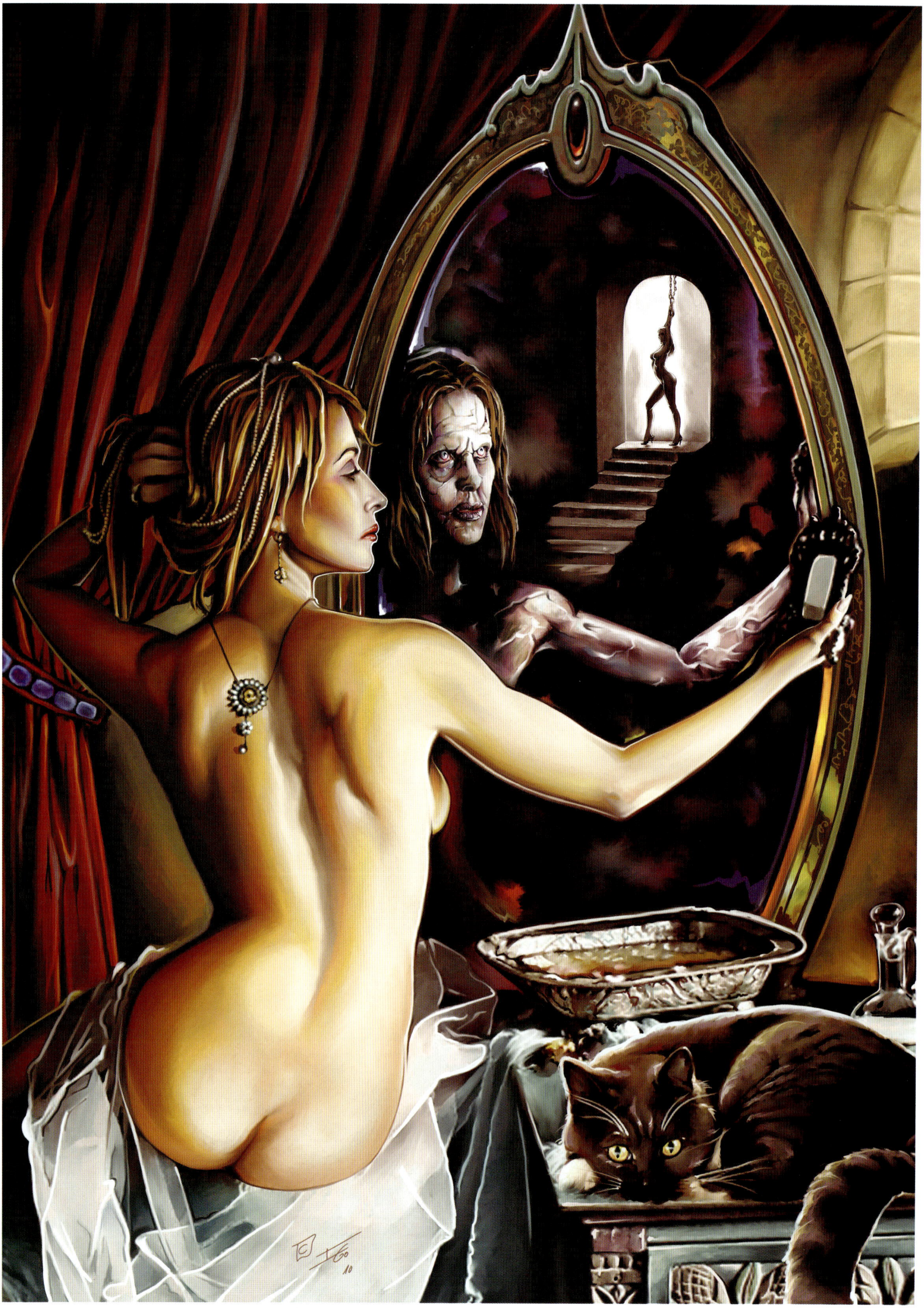

INAKI ORMAETXEA

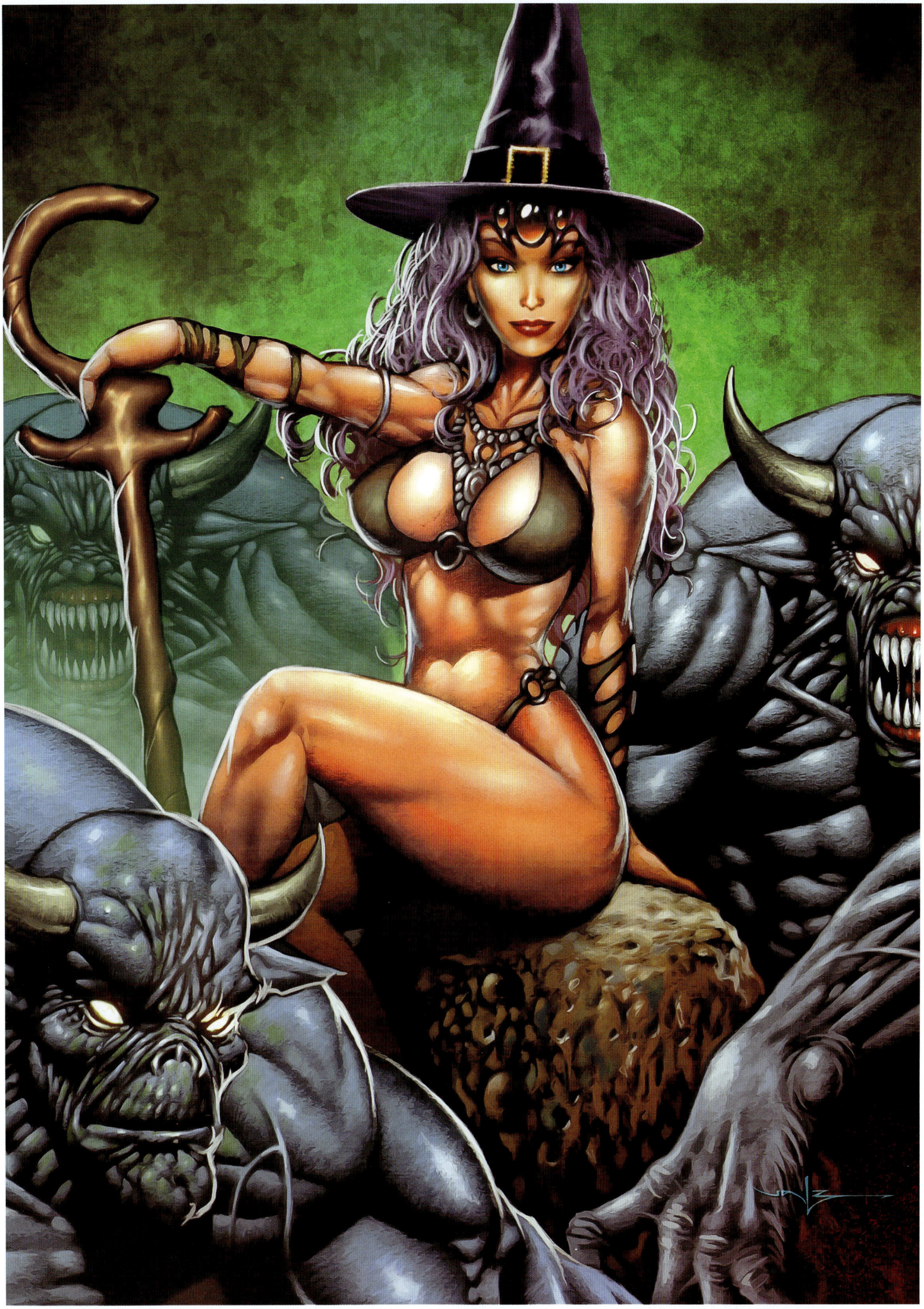

CARLOS VALENZUELA

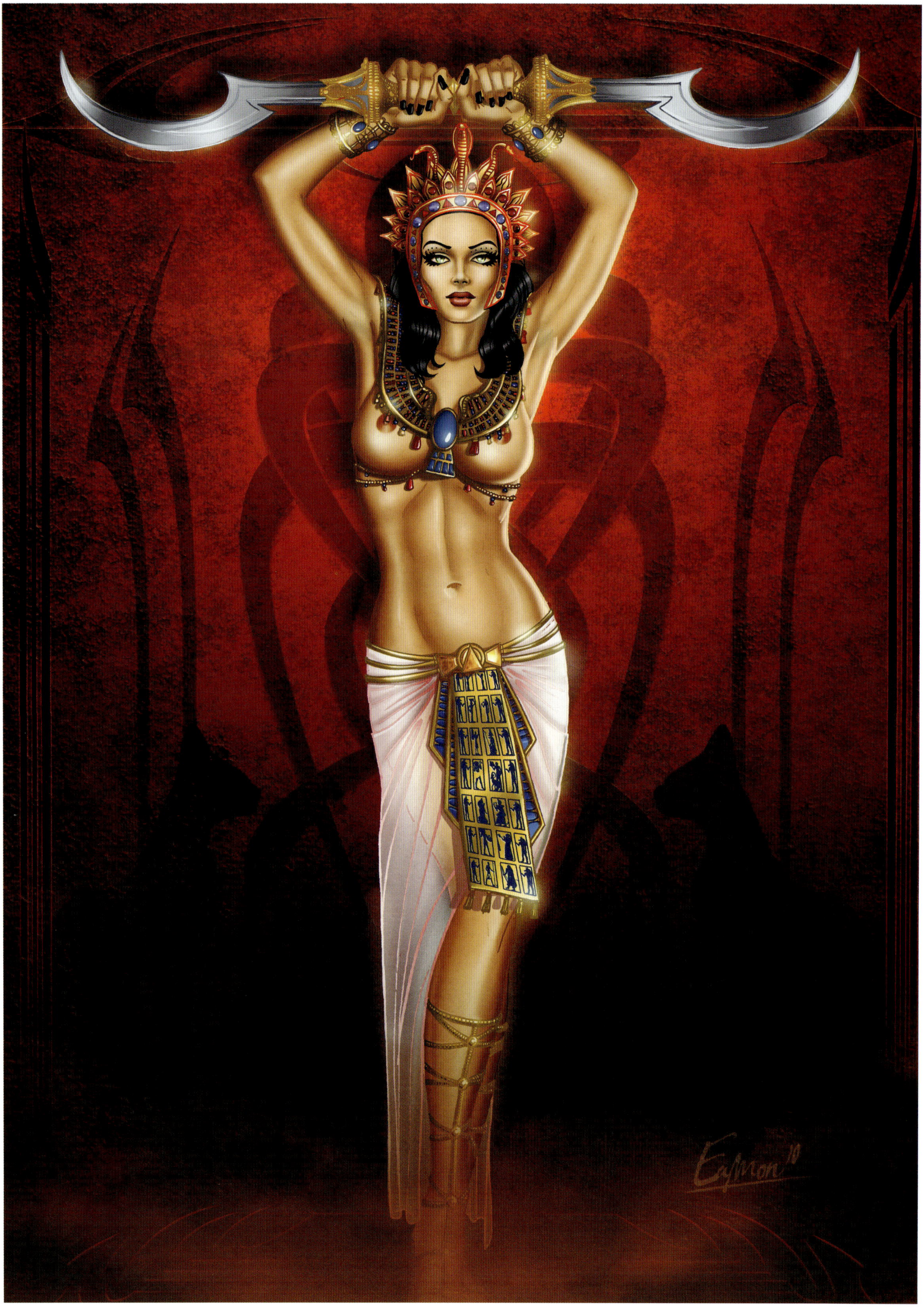

EAMON O'DONOGHUE

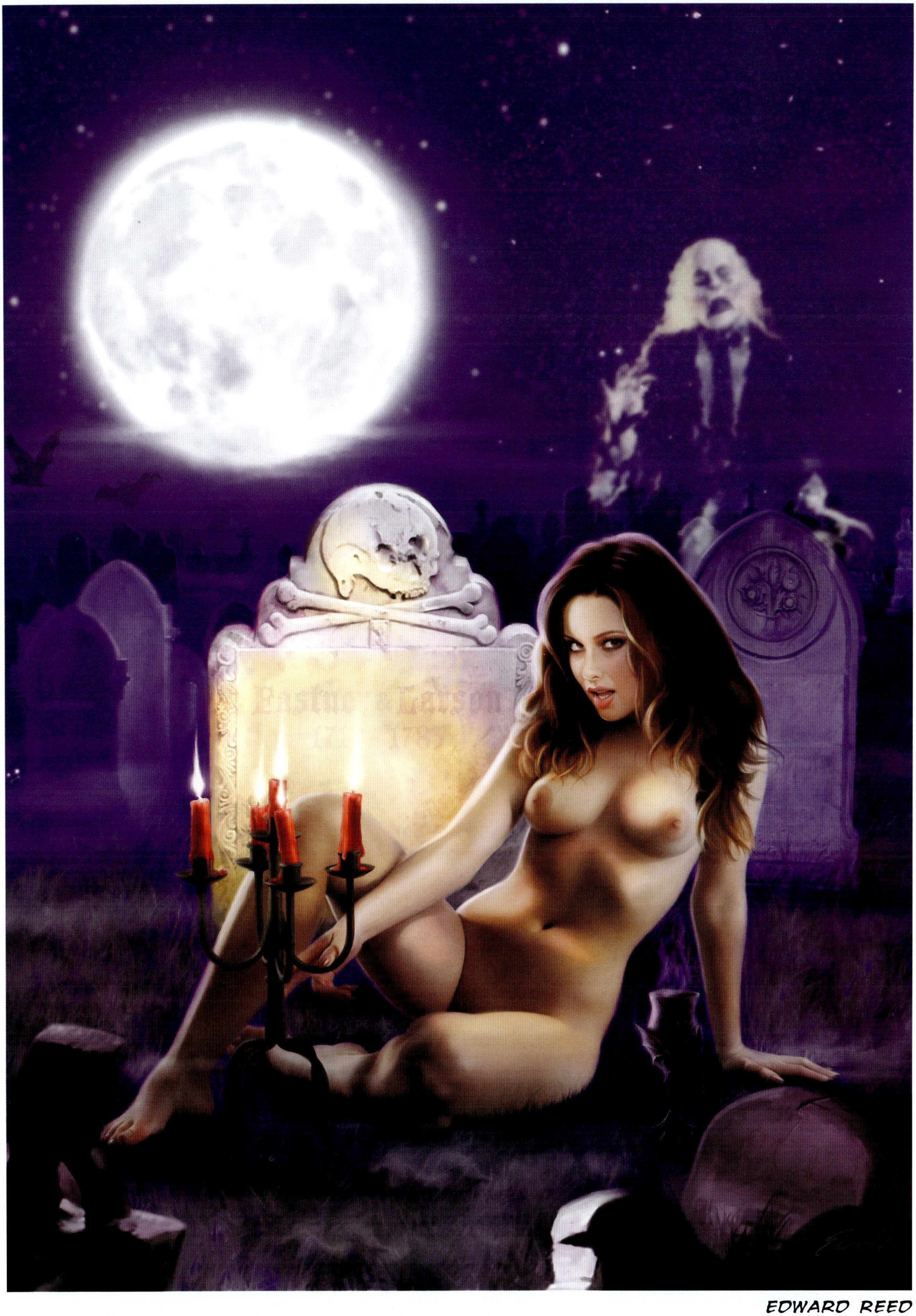

EDWARD REED

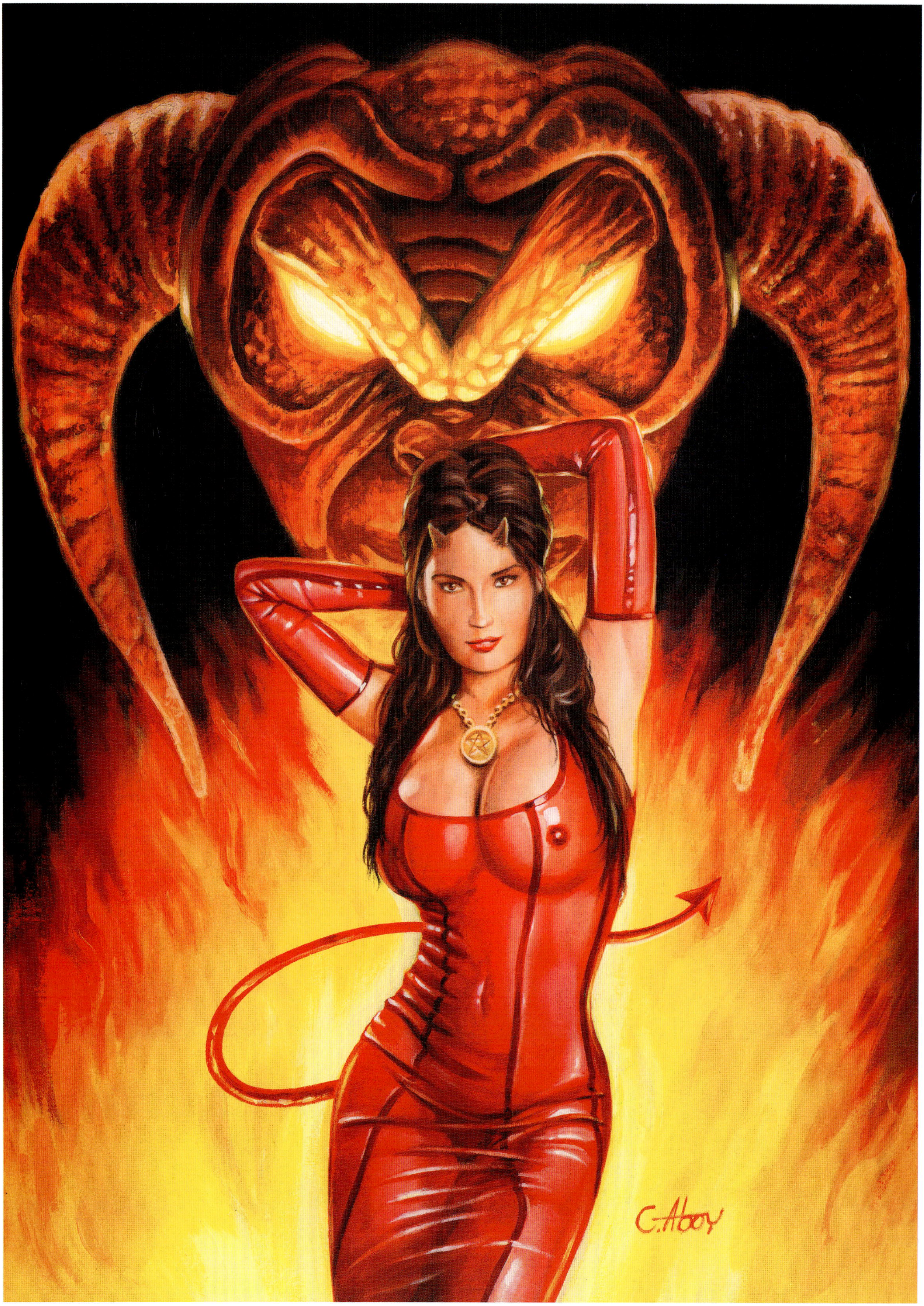

CLAUDIO ABOY

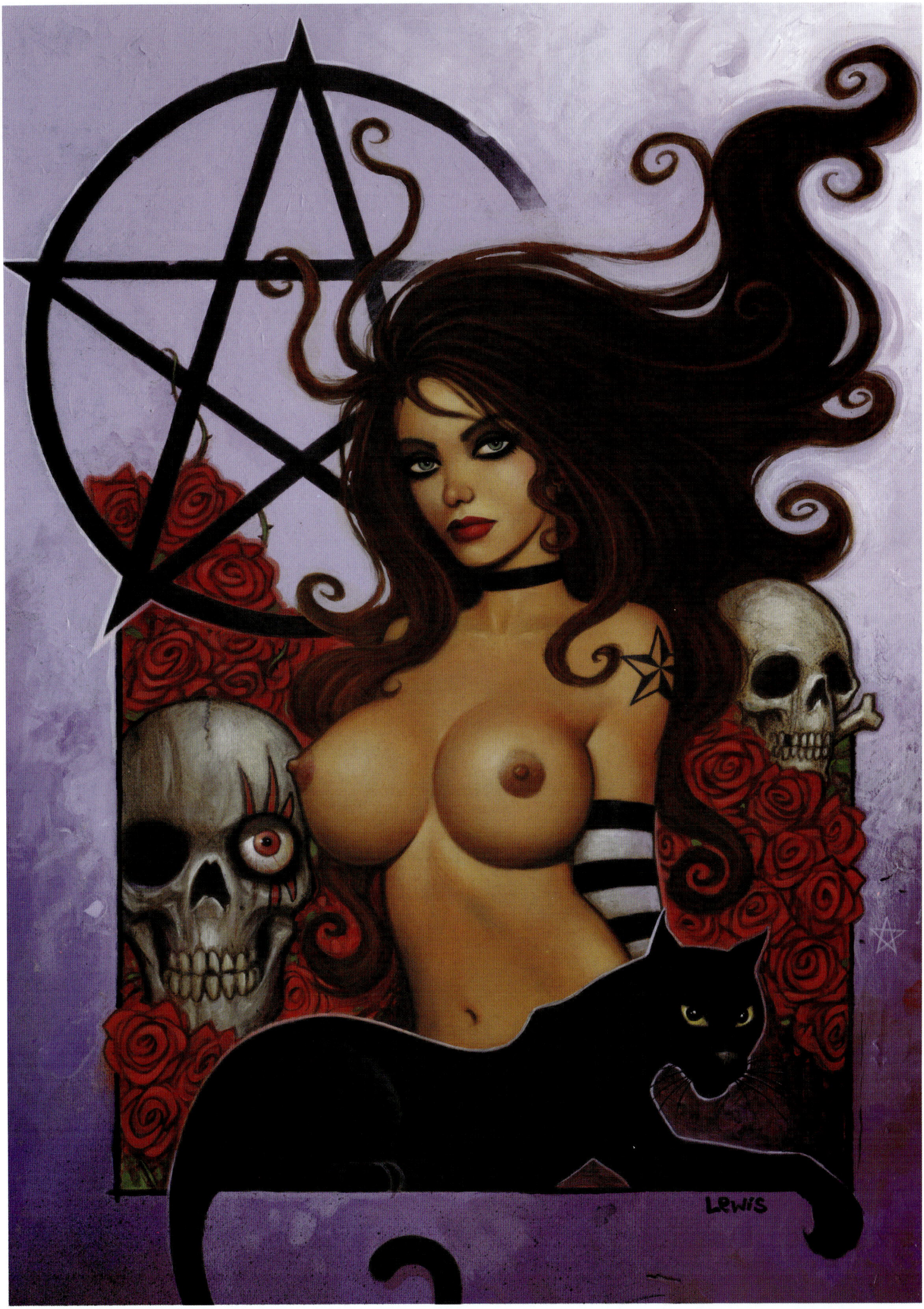

SCOTT LEWIS

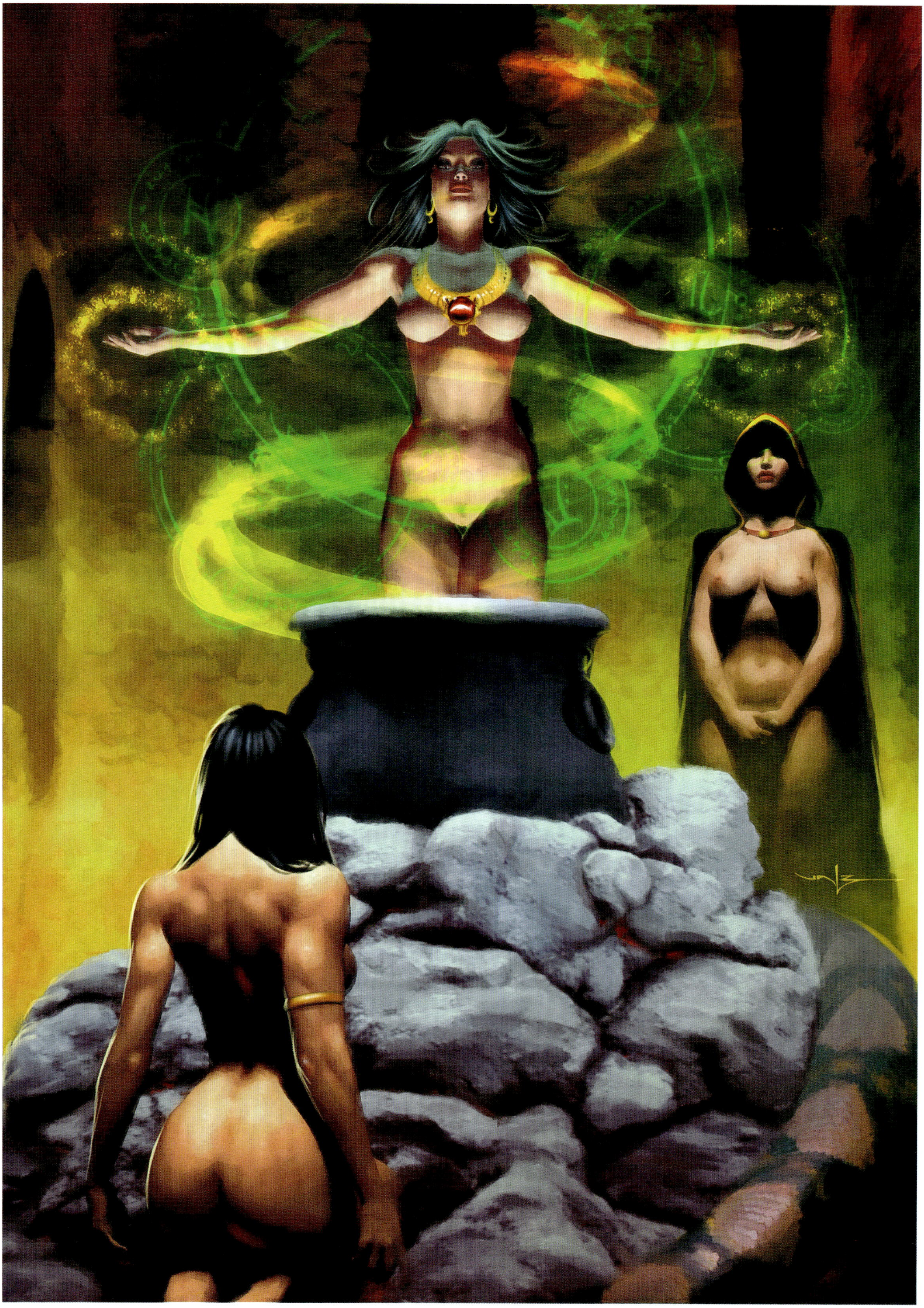

CARLOS VALENZUELA

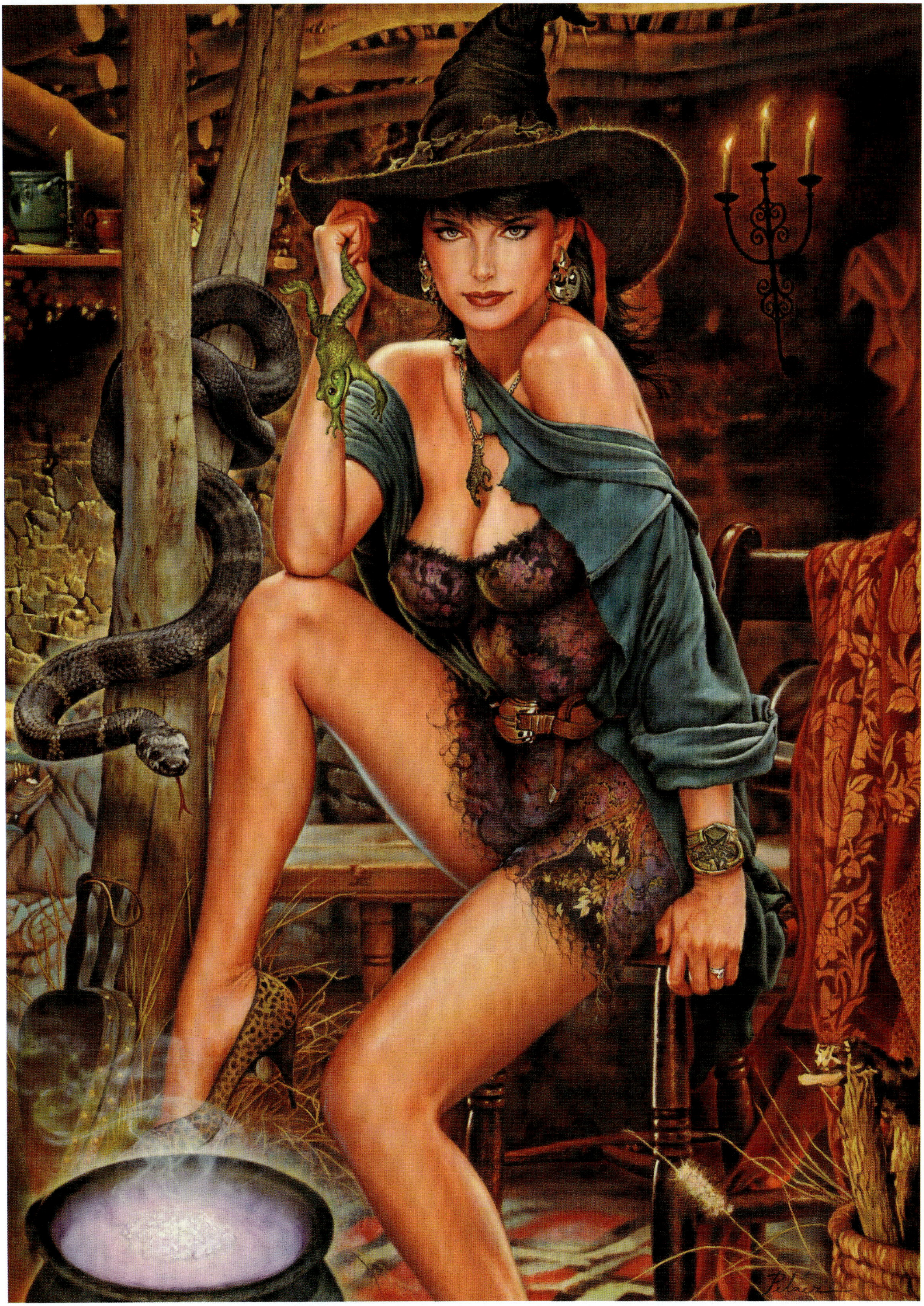

PELAEZ

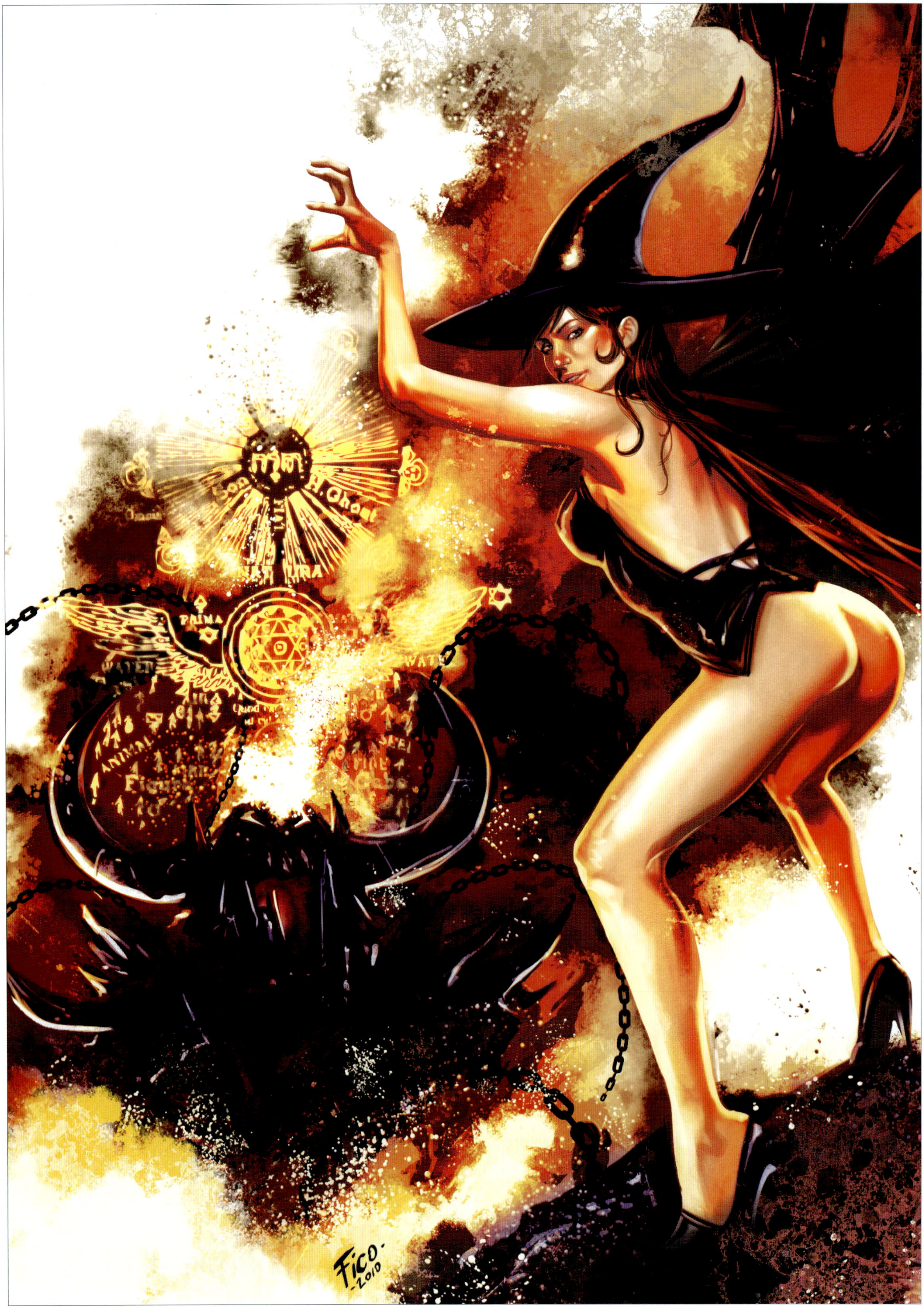

FEDERICO OSSIO

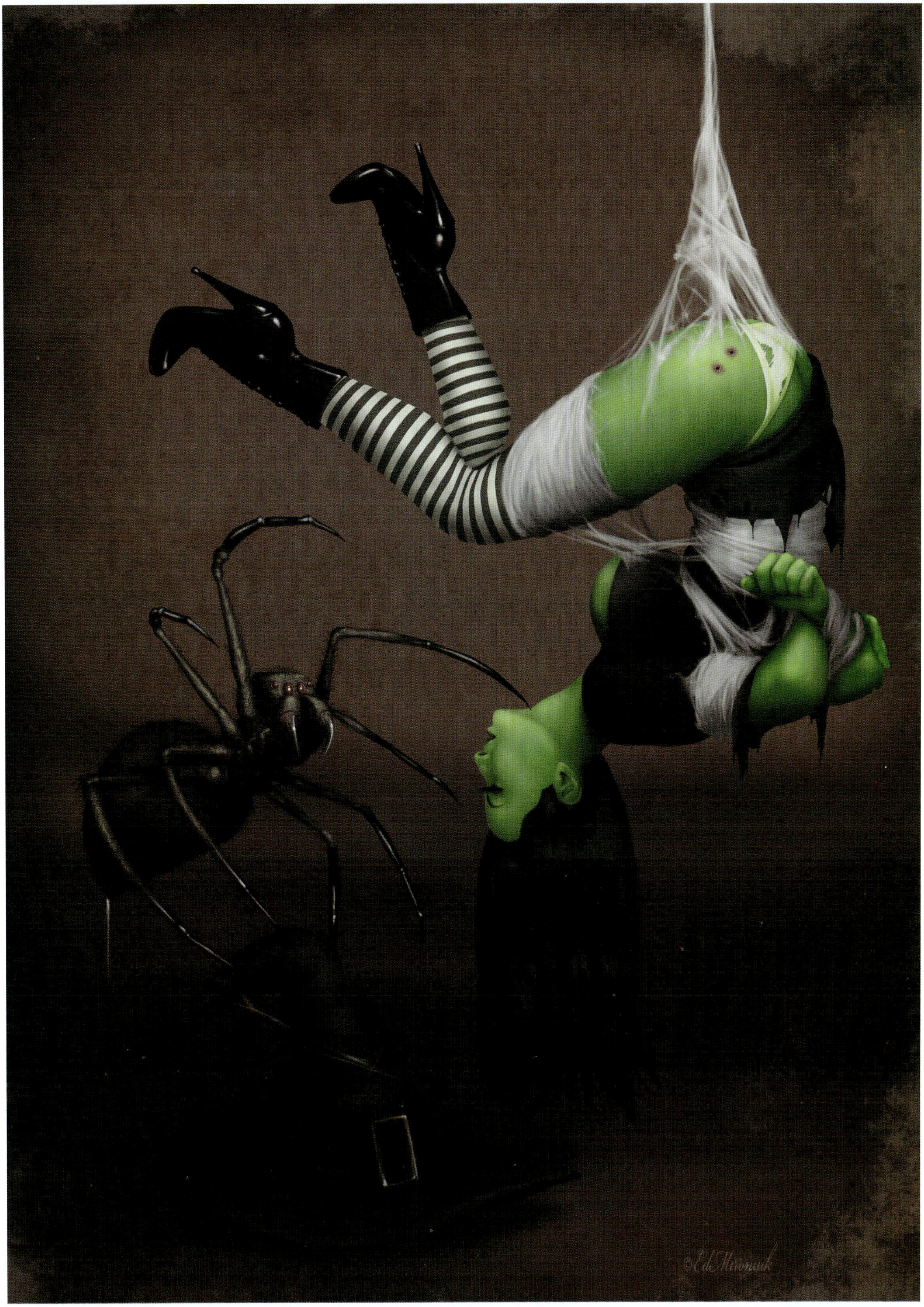

ED MIRONIUK

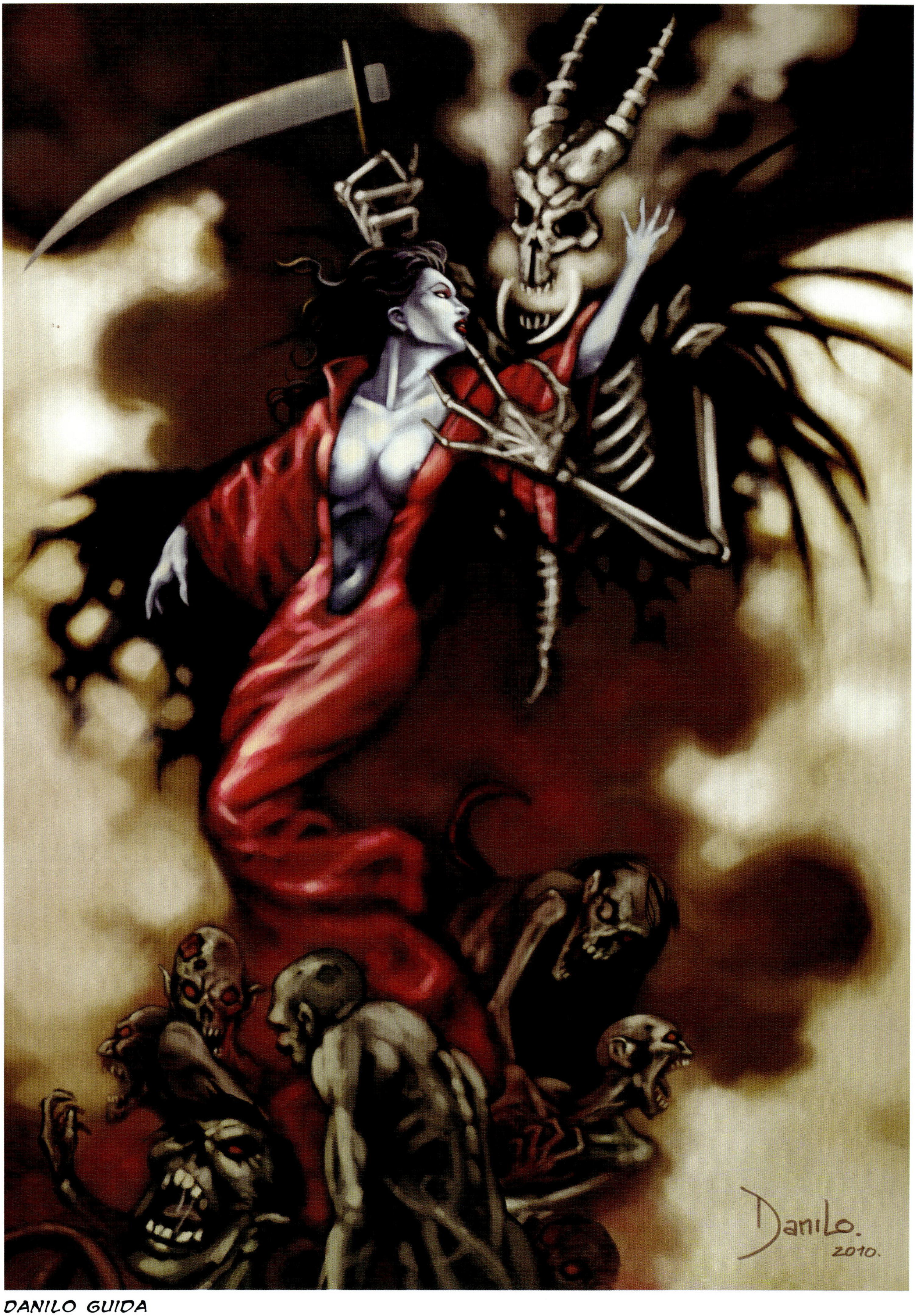

DANILO GUIDA

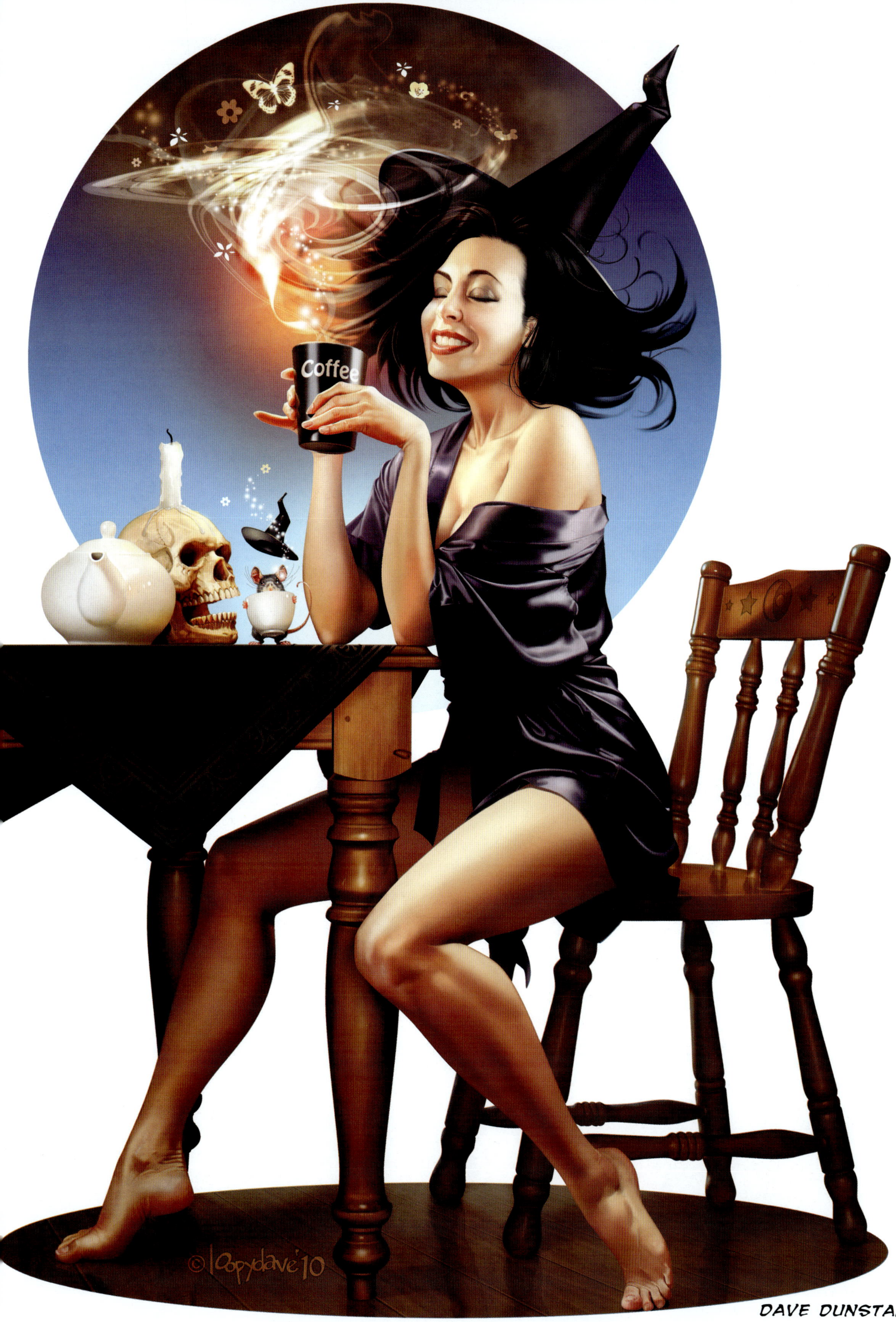

DAVE DUNSTAN

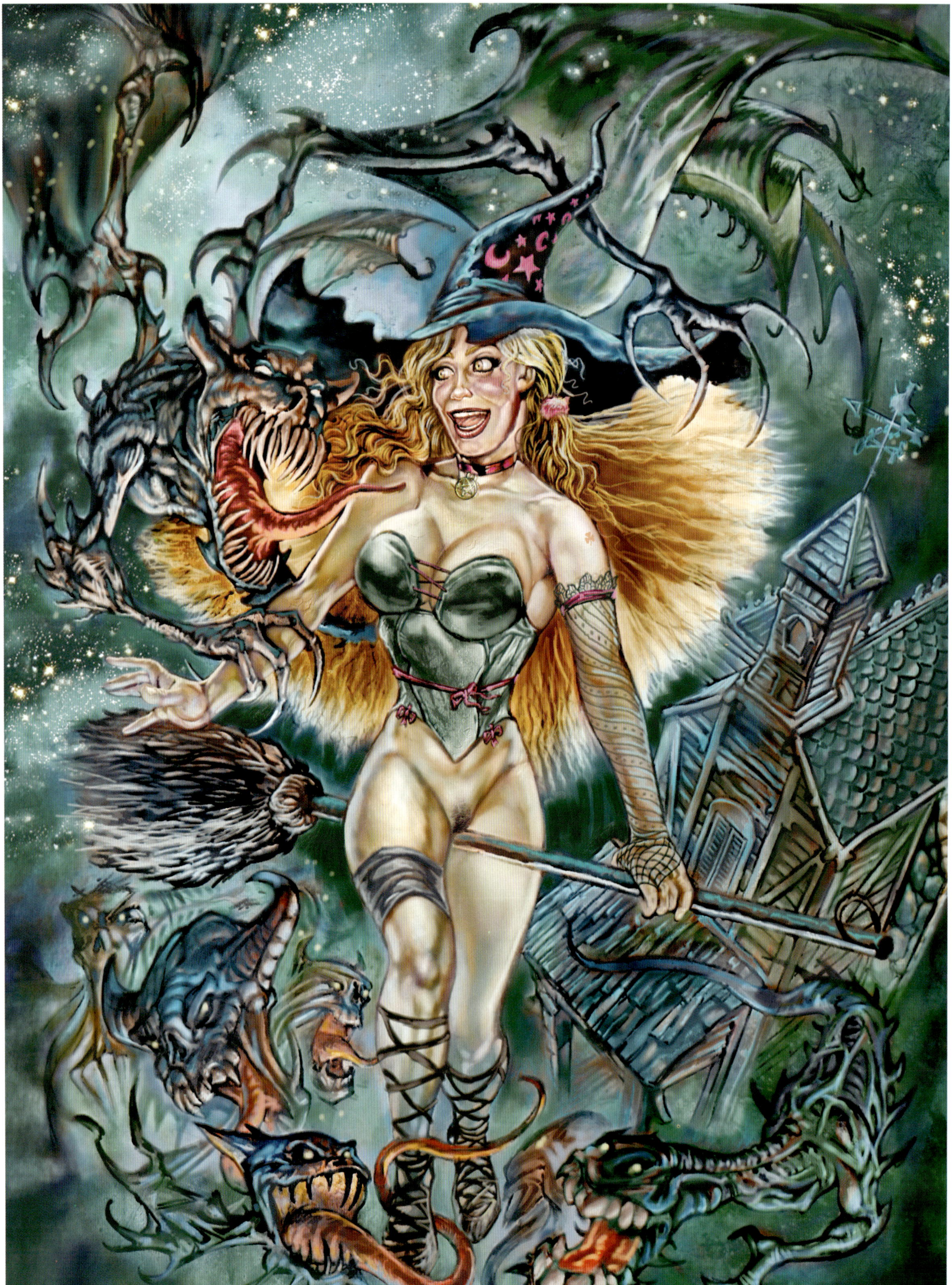

ANIBAL MARASCHI

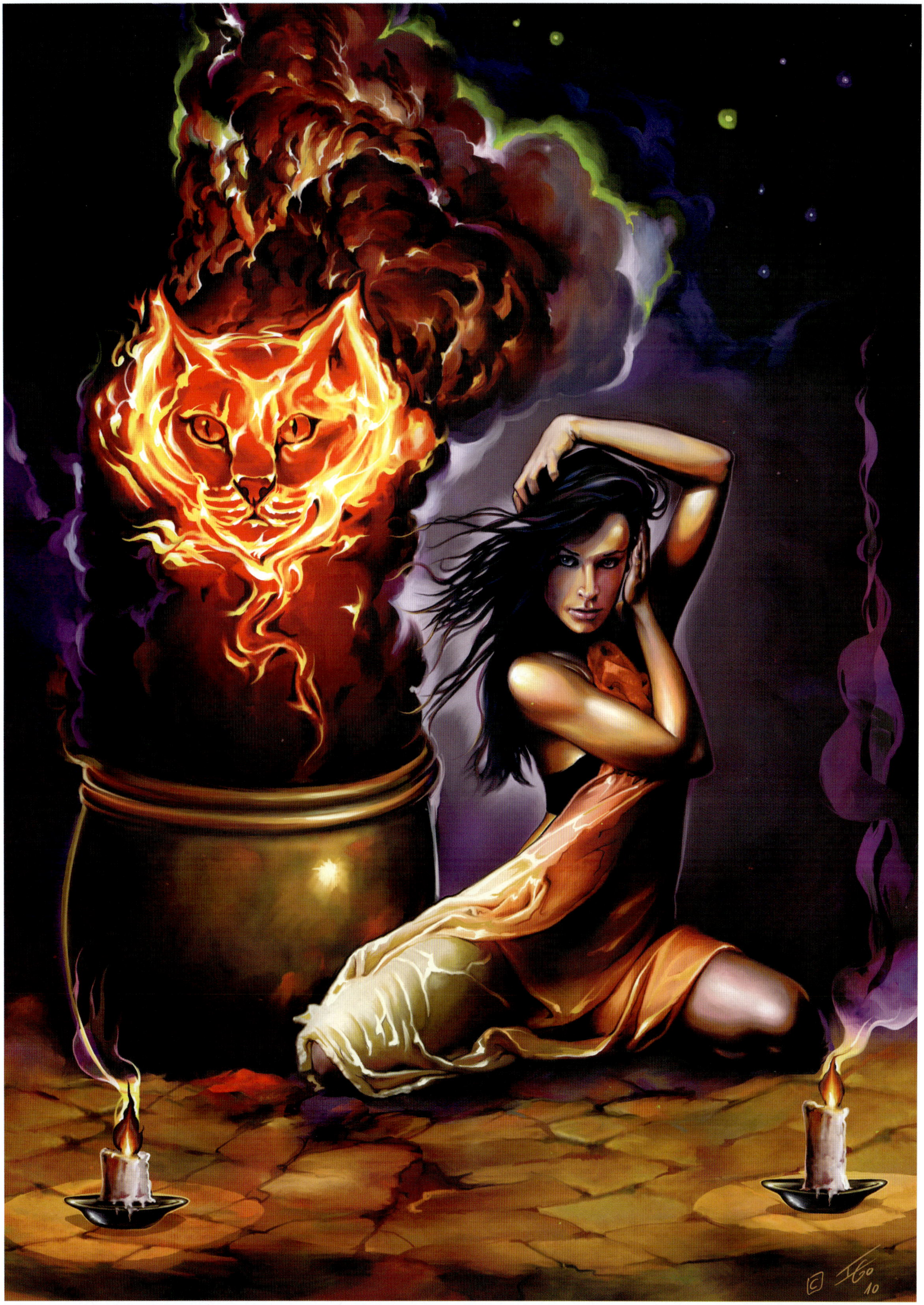

INAKI ORMAETXEA

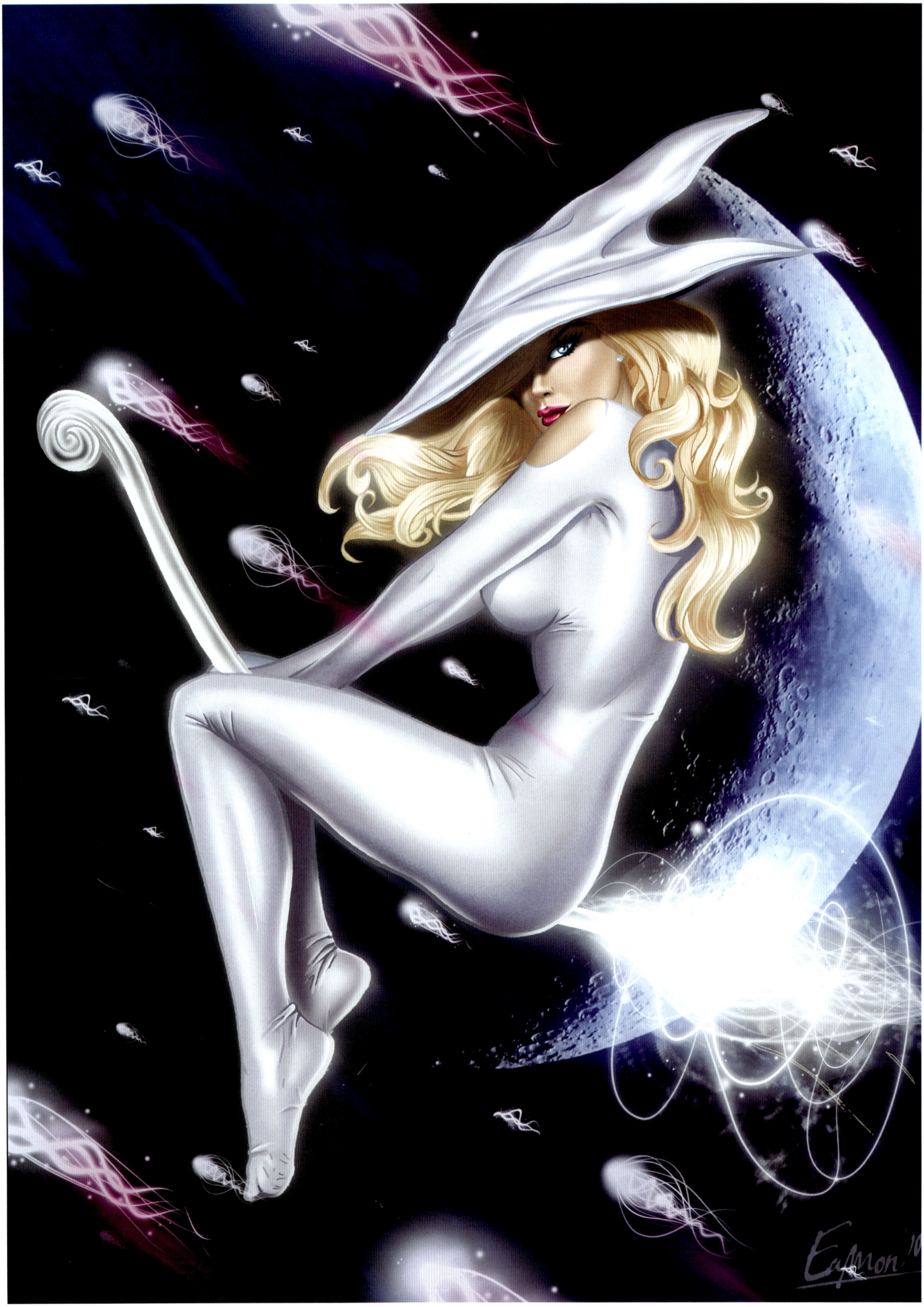

EAMON O'DONOGHUE

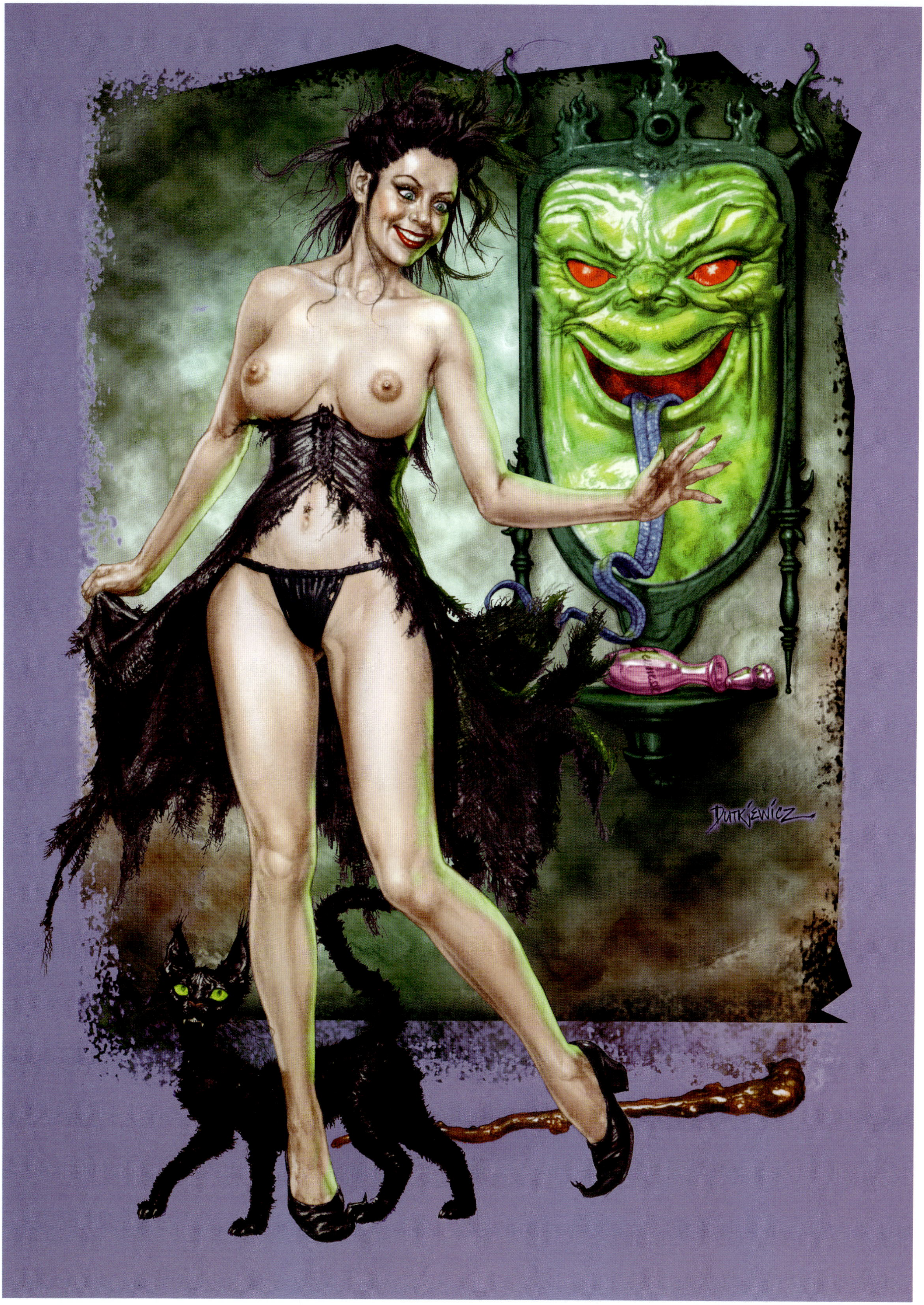

MICHAL DUTKIEWICZ

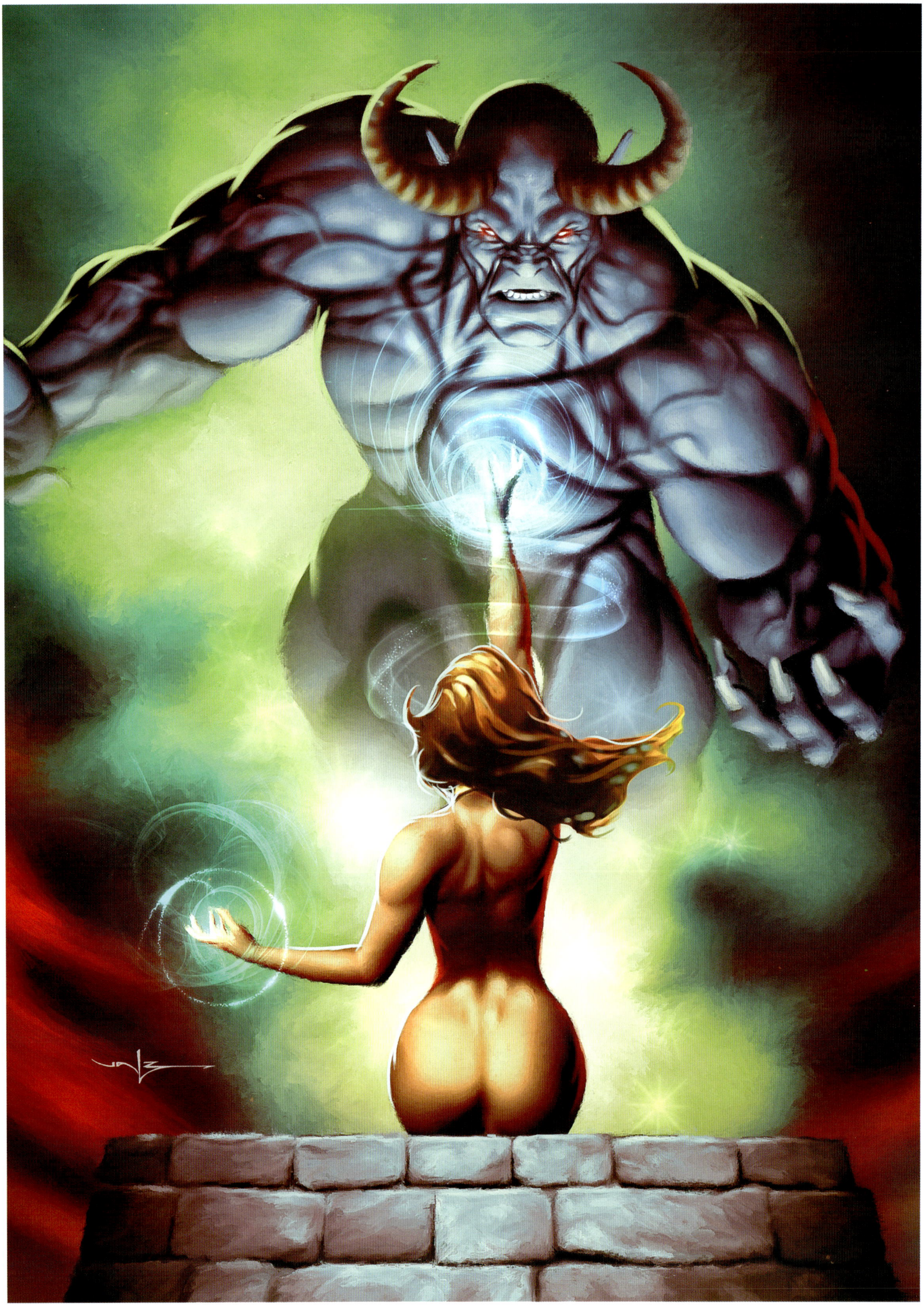

CARLOS VALENZUELA

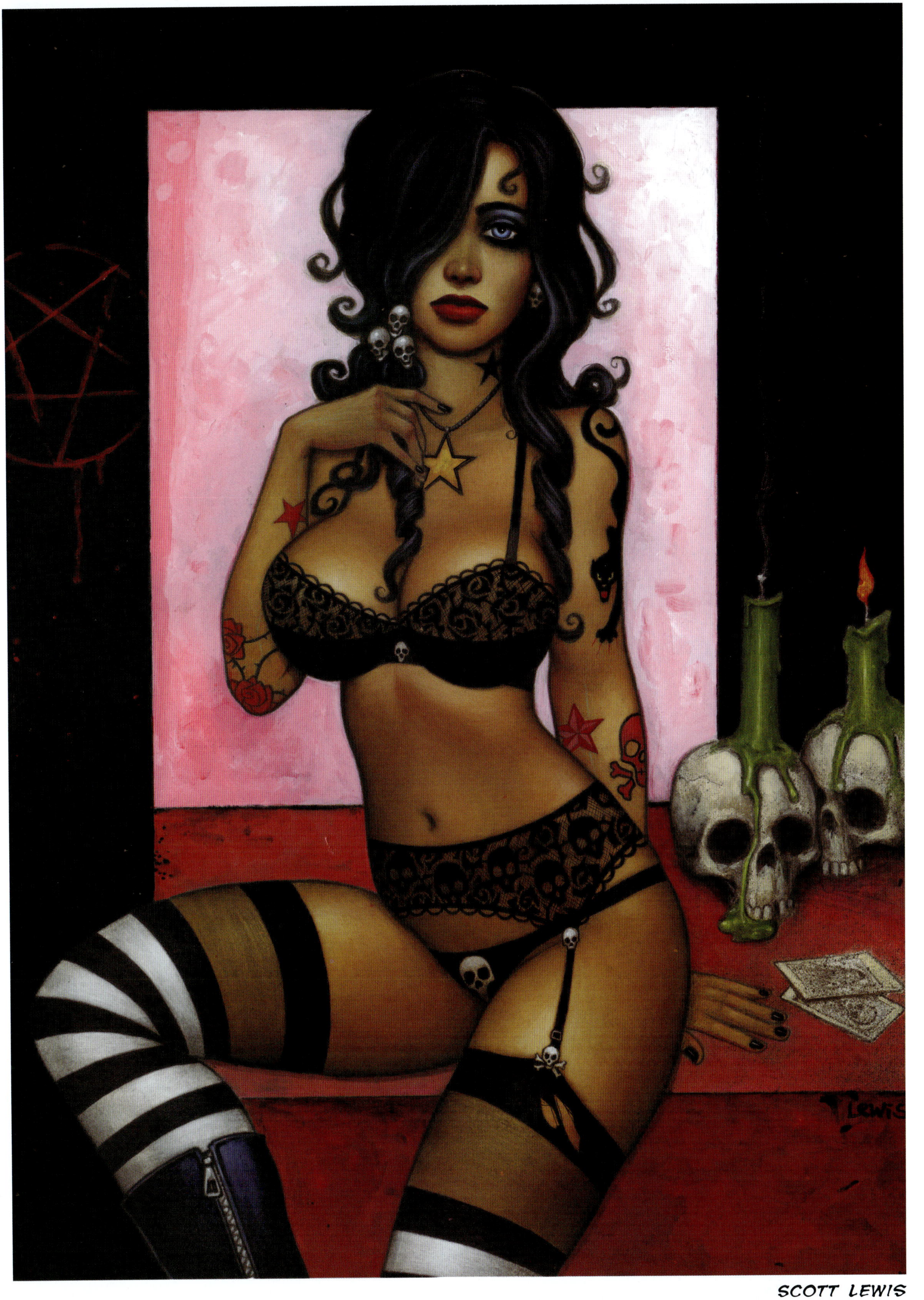

SCOTT LEWIS

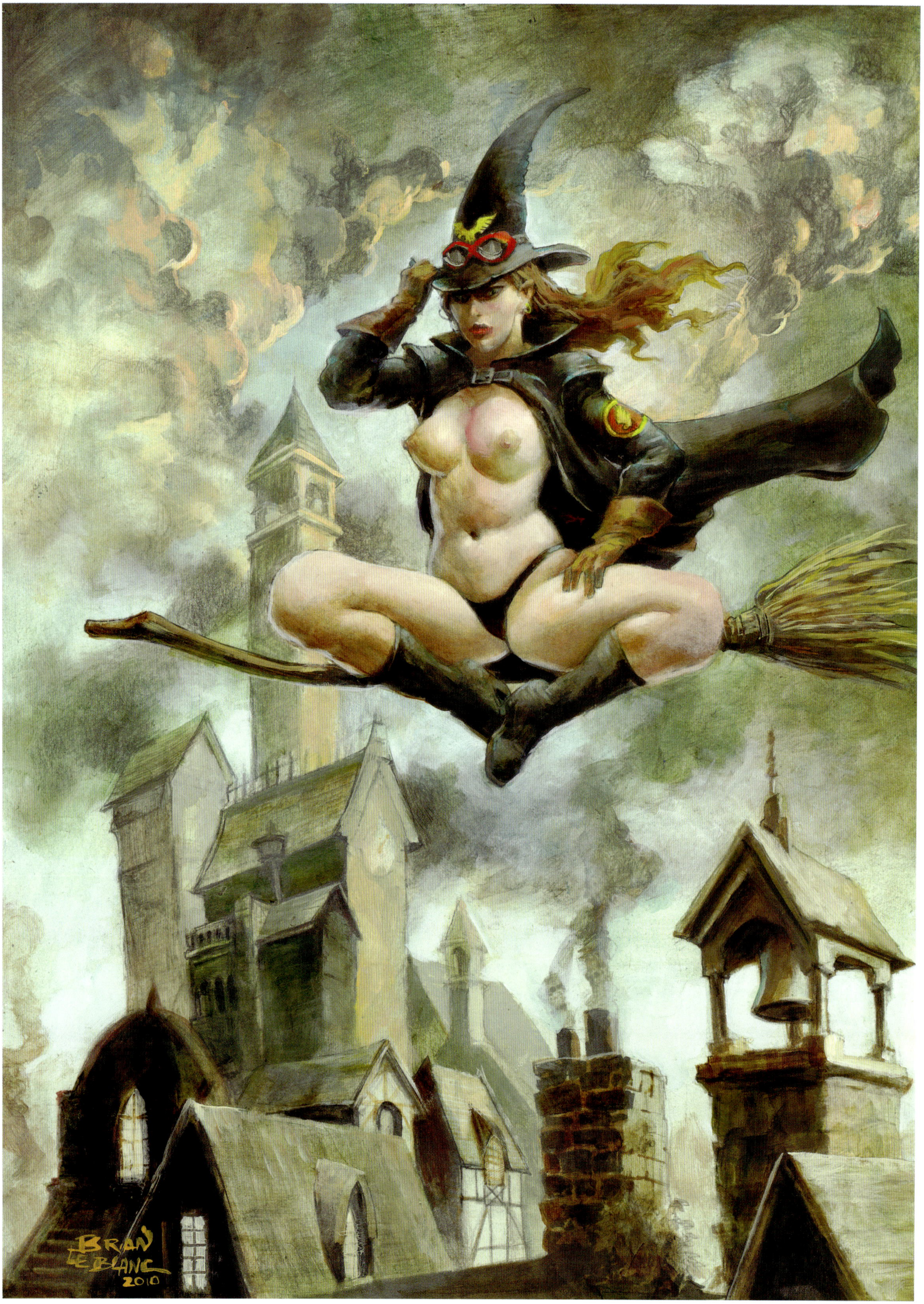

BRIAN LEBLANC

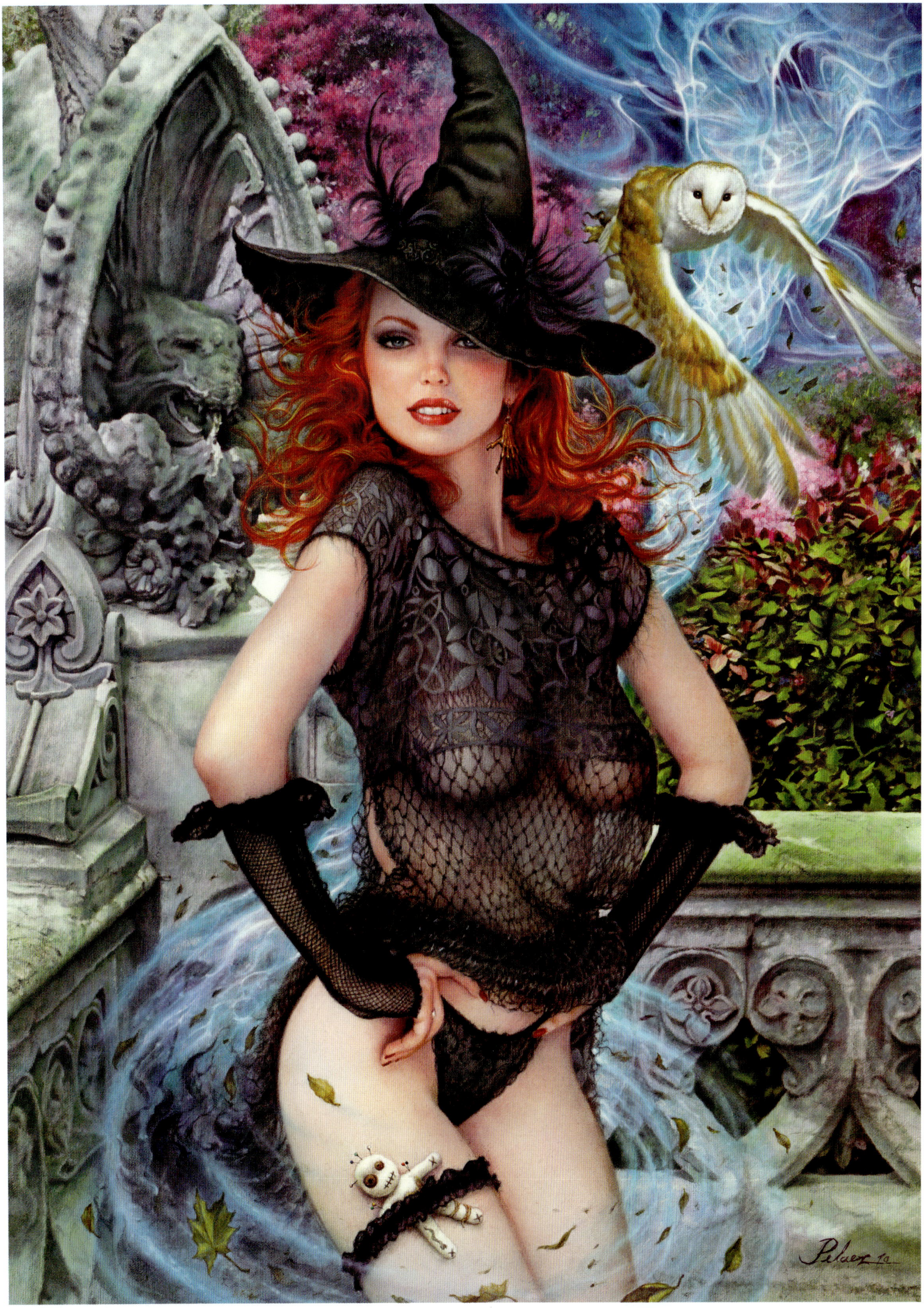

PELAEZ

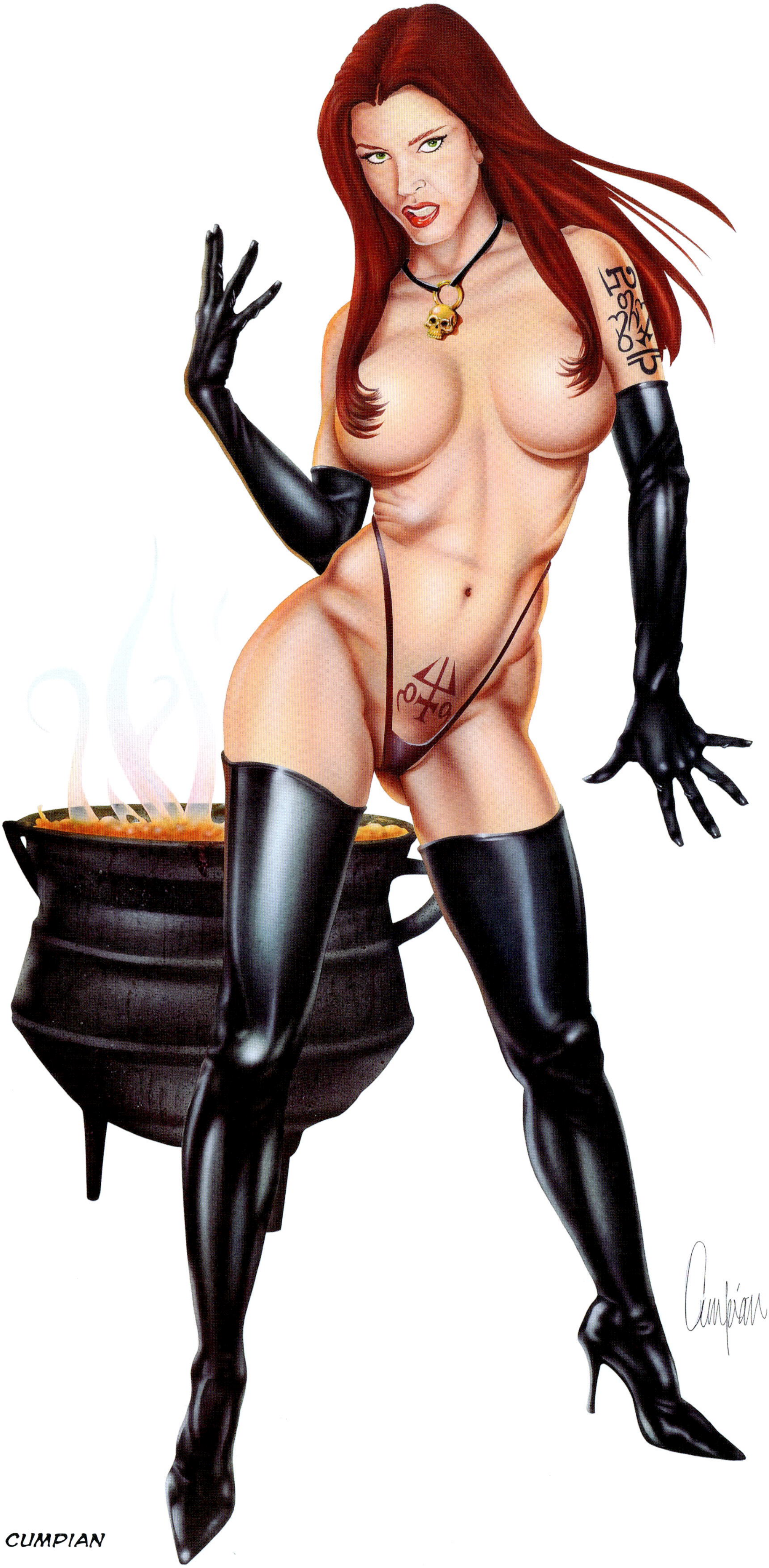

ERNESTO CUMPIAN

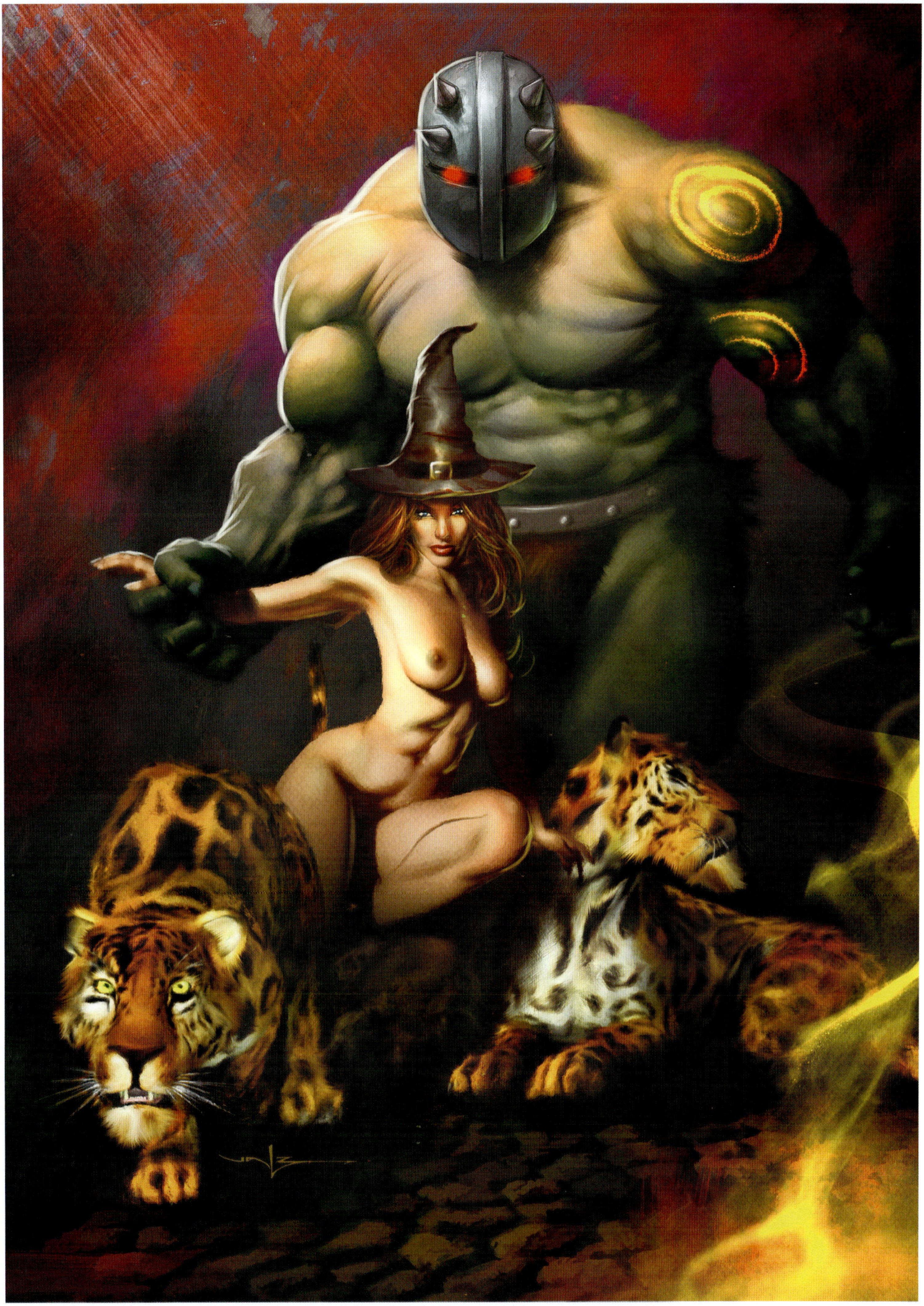

CARLOS VALENZUELA

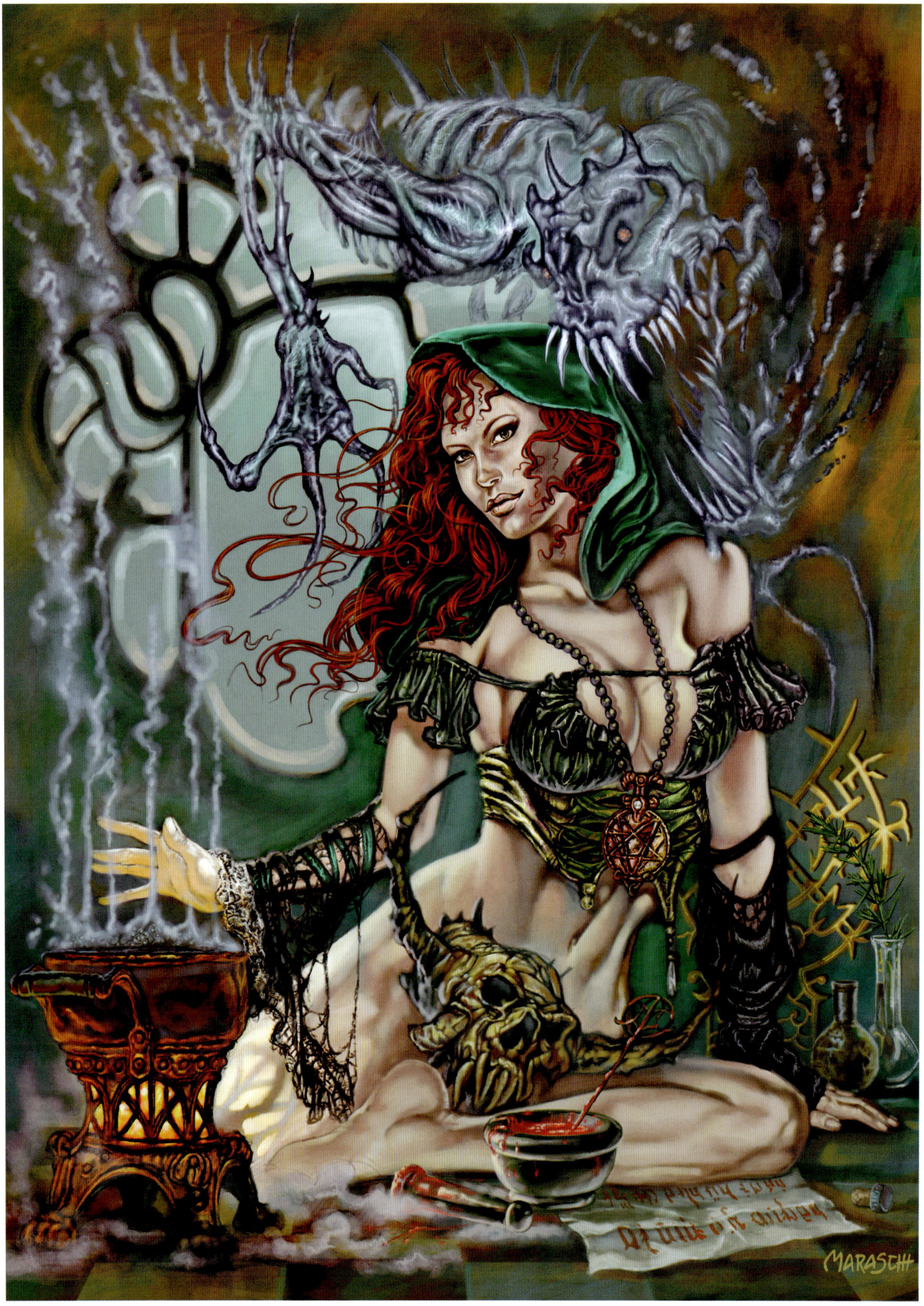

ANIBAL MARASCHI

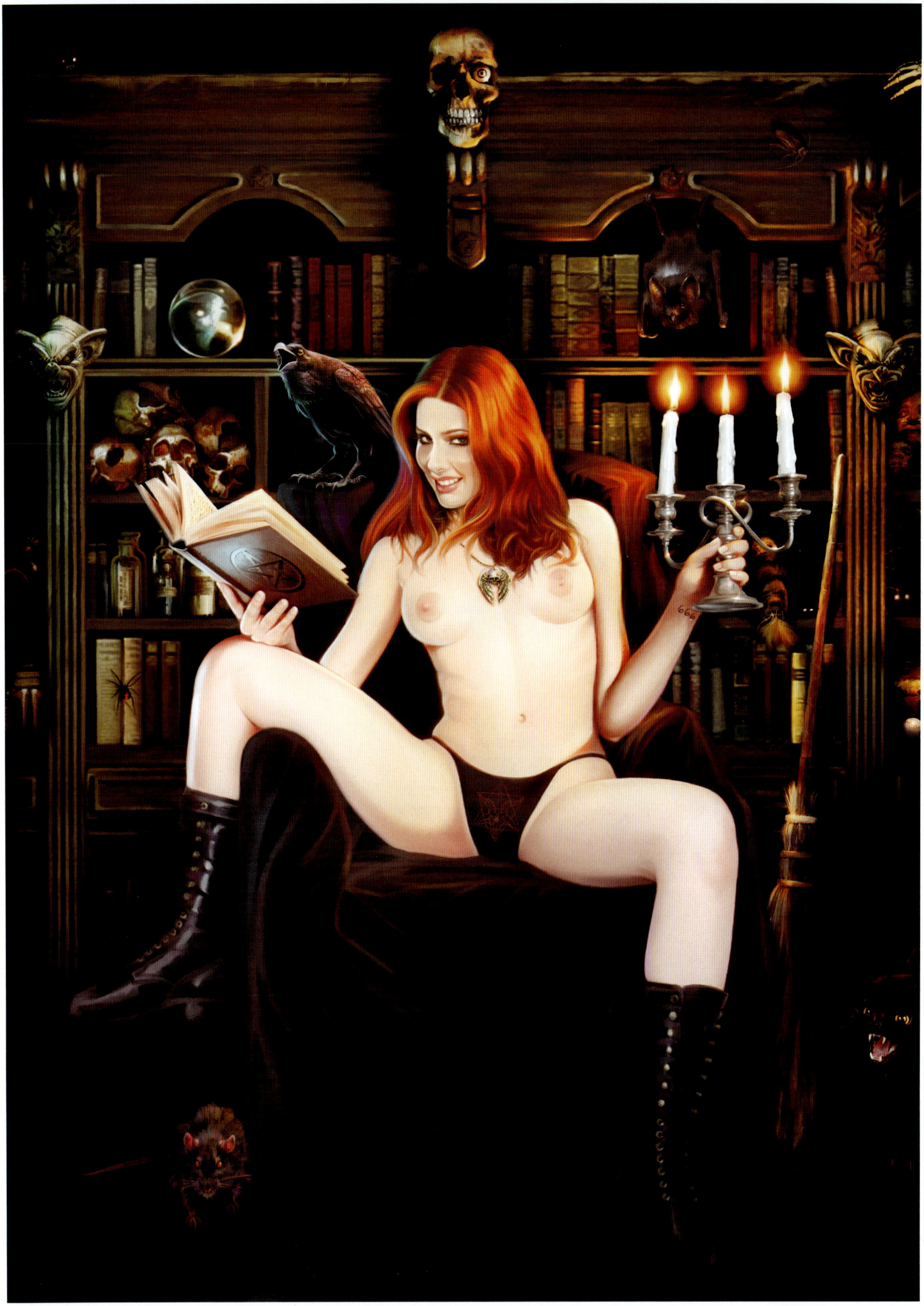

EDWARD REED

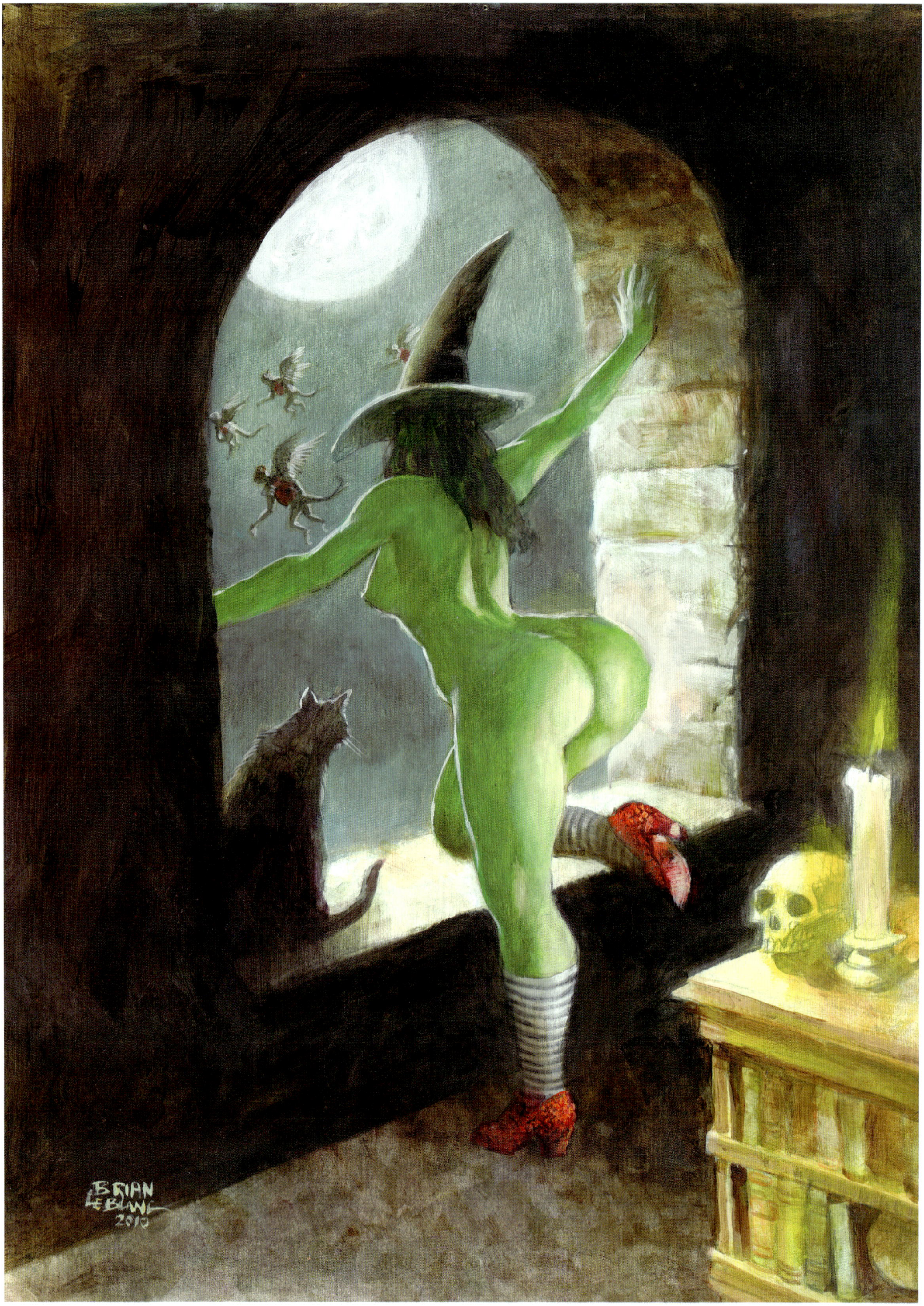

BRIAN LEBLANC